ENGLISH COUNTRY STYLE

MARY GILLIATT

Photography by
CHRISTINE HANSCOMB

Macdonald Orbis

For my father, Arthur Green, who loved the country
and made everything possible for me

A *Macdonald Orbis* BOOK

Text © Mary Gilliatt 1986
Design © Shuckburgh Reynolds Ltd 1986

First published in Great Britain in 1986 by Orbis Book Publishing
Corporation

Produced and designed by Shuckburgh Reynolds Ltd,
289 Westbourne Grove, London W11 2QA

This edition published by Macdonald & Co (Publishers) Ltd
London & Sydney

A member of BPCC plc
Reprinted in 1987

British Library Cataloguing in Publication Data
Gilliatt, Mary
    English country style.
    1. Interior decoration———England
    2. Country homes———England
    I. Title
    747.22   NK2043
    ISBN 0-356-1477-1

Designed by Carol McCleeve and David Fordham

Text drawings by Philip Hood
Drawings in chapter 9: colour by David Mallott; black and white by Ray Burrows

Typeset by SX Composing, Rayleigh, Essex
Reproduction by Aragorn Reproduction Co Ltd, London
Printed and bound in Italy by Mondadori Editore, Vicenza

Macdonald & Co (Publishers) Ltd,
Greater London House
Hampstead Road
London NW1 7QX

CONTENTS

INTRODUCTION   6

1 THE LURE OF THE ENGLISH COUNTRYSIDE   12

2 HALLS, LANDINGS AND STAIRCASES   34

3 SITTING ROOMS   66

4 LIBRARIES AND STUDIES   90

5 DINING ROOMS   108

6 KITCHENS   128

7 BEDROOMS AND CHILDREN'S ROOMS   146

8 BATHROOMS   176

9 ENGLISH COUNTRY STYLE IN PRACTICE   200

DIRECTORY OF SOURCES   214
   British Suppliers   214
   American Suppliers   217

FURTHER READING   219

INDEX   220

ACKNOWLEDGMENTS   223

INTRODUCTION

Such glorious clutter, *such splendid profusion of flowers and china, memorabilia and books, cooking utensils and dishes, such sheer exuberance is still as much a part of the English country theme as many simpler, quieter arrangements, for English style is nothing if not eclectic, nothing if not layered. Many of the hallmarks are here: the stripped pine dresser or hutch, the generous mix of flowers and foliage, the happy mixture of pink and blue, the pinboard completely hidden by the collected paperwork, the magpie collections of this and that.*

ver the past two decades there have been many books on English country houses and English style, or styles. Indeed, my first book, issued in 1967, was called *English Style* (Bodley Head) in Britain and *English Style in Interior Decoration* (Viking) in America, and dealt with the changes in interior decoration since the early 1950s and the Festival of Britain. Many of these books have been both lively and scholarly and have given detailed and fascinating accounts of the architecture and decoration of country houses as well as the kind of life led in them through the centuries. All of them have been handsome. I have gained much valuable knowledge and insight through reading Peter Thornton's encyclopedic and beautifully written *Authentic Decor: The Domestic Interior, 1620-1920*; Gervase Jackson-Stops' and James Pipkin's *The English Country House: A Grand Tour*; the wonderfully detailed and nostalgic books by Olive Cook, *English Cottages and Farmhouses* and *The English Country House*; John Cornforth's thought-

A deeply comfortable sofa *dominates more interesting furniture in this highly pleasing room. Lengths of lace filter the sun that pours through the long pine-framed windows with their integral panelled shutters. All woods are much the same colour here, so that the general effect is of a harmonious build-up of golden hues and tones. Nothing is over-obtrusive; even the harp's strong shape melds into the piano and the tallboy beyond, just as the various fabrics meld gently into each other.*

The white clapboard house *is so much a part of North America that one forgets the part it also plays in southern counties such as Kent and Sussex. In this particular instance the miniature size of the cottage is deceptive, for behind the higgledy-piggledy clapboard building is a courtyard flanked on one side by a converted barn and on the other by a modern wing built some two hundred years after the original structure. And who can blame the occupants for expanding on their particular bit of wooded land when they needed more space?*

The creeper, bereft of its softening leaves at the time of the photograph, is as much a part of many English country houses as a chimney. Note one major difference from American clapboard houses: the lack of shutters, which surrounded almost every American country window.

Greystone walls and slate tiles *blend with the greens of an English country house garden where red roses add just the right splash of colour.*

ful *The Inspiration of the Past* and, of course, Mark Girouard's incomparable *Life in the English Country House*.

But, having grown up in the heart of East Anglia, I wanted to illustrate in particular the rurality of English country house decoration, as well as its evolution to the English country style of today, and to explain how that style is achieved, using a representative group of lesser country houses, farmhouses and cottages to show the ways in which they relate to their surrounding countryside and also to their past. A general introduction on the lure of the countryside and its pervasive influence on the British is followed by short histories of each room within a house, which aim to explain in a simple way the roots of English country decoration and the reasons why certain colours, juxtapositions, arrangements and even objects are used today as a matter of almost unthinking tradition. The final chapter gives practical details of various decorational techniques for walls, floors, windows and furniture, which can achieve the effects illustrated and described previously, and is followed by a list of sources of English country style furnishings in Britain and the States.

Although the interiors of great country houses have been illustrated in some detail over the years and, thanks to dedicated restoration and reconstruction, have changed very little in substance, there has been comparatively little documentation of lesser country houses. Evidence can be gleaned from eighteenth- and nineteenth-century watercolours and the backgrounds in paintings of domestic scenes, and from the inventories of different estates in old auction house records. During the nineteenth century so many new houses were built that many of the old fell into appalling states of disrepair, and it is due to the sensitivity and knowledge of a hard core of enthusiastic restorers from the beginning of the century to World War II that so many beautiful examples of old manor houses survive. These enthusiasts managed to reintroduce that 'sense of remoteness in time', as John Cornforth put it in his *The Inspiration of the Past*, which happily is endemic to many country houses, and to bring a renewed awareness of the fabric and feeling of an old house, something which had been almost submerged in the waves of Edwardian philistinism.

This nucleus of enthusiasm, together with the endogenous English nostalgia, combined with what I believe to be an entirely new influence to produce the kind of decoration now thought of as thoroughly English. This new and unexpected influence was from the Americans who started to come to England from the late nineteenth century on. These civilized Americans with their sense of old values and traditions introduced a new dimension of comfort as well as sensitivity to the best of the past. John Cornforth quotes a Mrs Haweis, writing in *Beautiful Houses* (1882) about G.H. Boughton, an Anglo-American painter, friend of Whistler and Walter Crane, who was living in a house designed by Norman Shaw: 'He has brought from America a certain elegance of style in living which has not yet become common on this side of the Atlantic: less *posé* than French taste, more subtle than English. The prevailing impression of the house is softness, refinement, harmony. There is nothing *bizarre* or eccentric, to startle and not seldom annoy.'

Instead of buying the 'Queen Anne' style reproduction furniture of the Edwardian era, many people began to collect old pieces; to be delighted by the 'patina of age'; to try to make a synthesis of centuries. After the Second World War people who had inherited country houses determined to restore them, if not to full grandeur, at least to a semblance of former glory, and many other people looked for country houses to buy and restore, from derelict manors to broken-down barns and farms to unmodernized cottages. Few houses today are restored and furnished with the meticulous attention to detail and period, the kind of freezing of history typical of the romantic restoration of the first third of the century. People now usually think of English country style as in part the 'humble elegance' of John Fowler, the kind of style that draws elements from every facet of the past that seem best suited to create a relaxed and harmonious whole, whatever the period of the house. Most important, it is a style that fits comfortably with the surrounding landscape.

Mary Gilliatt

A peaceful green setting *outside to complement the interior: French windows open from the living room on to a flagstone path, with honeysuckle and roses by the door.*

CHAPTER ONE

THE LURE OF THE ENGLISH COUNTRYSIDE

Garden into landscape *The British have always excelled at the careful siting of country houses (apart from the many early ones that do not have a south-facing aspect, a relic of the days when the south winds were supposed to carry the plague). The scene pictured left, with the church at the rear and horses to the front grazing contentedly amongst the daisies, is the kind of rural idyll that most English people dream of seeing from their windows, especially if their gardens happen to merge imperceptibly into the fields and meadows beyond.*

T he difference between quintessentially English country and everybody else's country is not just the difference in colour or terrain, the quality of the light or the intensity of the heat. It is not just in the tangle of varying greens, the damp freshness of the foliage after rain, the sweetness of the early morning birds. The Dordogne, Umbria, Virginia, New England, are all a joyous weft and warp of green in season, their trees magnificent, their birds exotic.

It is not just in the meandering lanes, hedges thick with wild rose and hazel, oak saplings and holly, rickety gates opening on to meadows drizzled with buttercups. There are parts of America's East Coast, delights like Block Island, Rhode Island, where the lanes and stone walls out-Devon Devon and the scent of the honeysuckle hedges is so piercingly sweet it intoxicates.

It is not just in the lovely sounds and scents of a summer weekend with its mixture of wood pigeons warbling, late cocks crowing, grass-

An ancient churchyard *and sheep grazing among the tombstones by a tiny East Anglian church – a country house view that is unchanging, peaceful, charming.*

A clock tower *in a fringe of trees is a familiar sight in English villages. White-painted windows and white-painted gates add a feeling of well-tended prosperity to the whole.*

hoppers sawing, bees buzzing, remote tennis balls thudding, all mingled with the smell of warmed lime leaves and hay, night-scented stocks and new-mown grass. The scorched, aromatic afternoons of Provence, Frangipani in the Australian bush, lazy afternoons dabbling on the great American lakes, are equally heady.

It is not just in the cold, clear autumn nights when wood smoke tinges the sharp air and the stars outshine the mellower lights of the villages. Night skies in Arizona, the Middle East, Africa, Australia, Tuscany, are infinitely more majestic.

Nor is it in the tumbledown barns, the wide grassy rides through brambly woods, the slow, willow-fringed, green-brown rivers. Barns all over New England, the Mid-West and the Southern States of America are handsome, coveted buildings. The groupings of French and Italian farm buildings are a delight. Woods and rivers almost everywhere are on a more spectacular scale.

It is much more, I think, the very lack of drama in the English countryside, the gentleness, the pervading green and earth tones

Stone walls, stone paths, *merge into each other, softened by the varying greens of lawns, and trees and shrubs. This blend of tawny greys and greens is typical of the Cotswolds and the West country. Here, the grouping of roofs and the surrounding framework of walls is an echo of the medieval fortified manors.*

14

under a great bowl of water colour sky. It is the way you come across an old wisteria-covered house at the bend of a lane, moulded by years into an intricate design with its surrounding garden. It is the sight of a wobbly ruddy-tiled roof and wafting chimneys through a fold in the hills; the glimpse of decayed but dignified tawny Cotswold stone up a mossy drive, or a pair of chestnut Suffolk Punches grazing under a dipping oak. Above all, it is the kind of haphazard dependability of it all – the sense of only occasionally fractured continuity.

Inviting meadows stay inviting when you climb over the gate and picnic there. The grass really is as soft as it looks, not disappointingly rasping like those bright green swards in the West Indies which look, at first sight, so velvety. And you will not get bitten by anything harsher than an ant, a bee, a wasp, or a mosquito. Insects, and what reptiles there are, are as generally laid-back as their surroundings.

The rhythm of the seasons is immutable. The landscape changes with the scars furrowed by twentieth-century communication systems, but not, all things considered, so very much. One of the

Drystone walls, *sleepy dog allowed to lie and hazy views: all the ingredients of English country style.*

15

An old farmhouse *that is as haphazard and rambling as the house pictured opposite is neat. The one seems literally to grow out of the land, the other seems to have been gently fitted in.*

extraordinary things about the British Isles is the great tracts of land that remain uninhabited. Walk in Northumberland, for example, and the sheep-shorn hills stretch unmolested by progress. Hadrian's Wall is a good deal more decrepit than in Roman times, but has much else changed?

Elsewhere, villages look much the same as they must have done for generations: a farm, a clutch of brick or stone and half-timbered cottages, a church and a mill, a big house or two comfortably enclosed in their undulating parks, perhaps a river and a green. Only the straggling fringe of council houses around the edges proclaims the age, with the difference that most of the original villagers are probably now living in the new housing, while internally their cottages are likely to be changed beyond recognition for weekend dwellers who are much more determinedly rural than the rustics. Nostalgia is England's aesthetic strength and its political weakness, but it is all-pervasive. The decoration of the greater percentage of English country houses today, whatever their size, whatever their period, is based on nostalgia and there is much to be nostalgic about – not least the contrast of all the country house stood for and our own uncertainties, the stability and certainty of life then and our own uprootedness.

A comfort born of continuity

The point is, of course, that since Cromwell, the British have been extraordinarily lucky in their freedom from civil wars and disturbing invasions. This comparative peacefulness over so many centuries has led to many houses and estates remaining in the hands of the same families. The changes and re-buildings, embellishments and down-turns that tend to follow such a pattern have given the English house a diversity which is hardly equalled elsewhere, a diversity held together

A foreground of daffodils, *swans on a symmetrical pool, a neatly balustraded, neatly fenestrated grey brick house with fields falling away in the background: these are part of an historical blend of ingredients that are endemic to England. Houses like this manage to look carefully executed yet an innate part of the landscape, as carefully tended as the lawns blending into the shaggy grass and trees.*

Ivy-covered brickwork, *rosy garden walls, summer houses and rustic hideaways are as quintessentially English as the proverbial lawns and the herbaceous borders. Here, the stone griffins on their pillars guarding the wooden bench in front of the patched-up archway are redolent of that "simultaneous look of relaxed elegance and benign neglect" that the writer and critic John Richardson so succinctly describes.*

by long strands of continuity which in turn have tended to give a sense of security and serenity to surrounding villages and the lesser houses in the area.

It is not surprising then, that the interiors both of English country houses and of houses in the country – for there is a distinction in grandeur – seem to have absorbed the same comforting comfort, the same relaxed haphazardness, the same mellowness and gentleness. There is nothing dramatic, nothing manicured or deliberately decorated about English country style with its "simultaneous look of relaxed elegance and benign neglect", as the writer and critic John Richardson so succinctly put it.

Vita Sackville-West, who grew up in one of the most splendid of ancient English houses, Knole, the Sackville family house in Kent, and who herself created the hauntingly beautiful gardens at Sissinghurst, wrote that "the peculiar genius of the English country house lies in its knack of fitting in". In fact, this melding of nature and architecture which we now take for granted as an integral part of the English

Nature is constrained *behind the peripheral wrought iron gates and brick garden wall. Yet typically the gates seem a rather arbitrary intervention between tracts of inviting grass, a gentle barrier across a soft green landscape dissolving into a great bowl of sky.*

landscape was an eighteenth-century innovation and ironically it started not in the country but in London.

In 1734, a Sir Thomas Robinson, reporting on the great success of the new garden designed by William Kent for Frederick Prince of Wales, at the early Carlton House, London, announced that "there is a new taste in gardening just arisen which has been practised with so great success in the Prince's gardens in town, that a general alteration of some of the most considerable gardens in the kingdom is began". It had, he said, "the appearance of beautiful nature".

Revelling in nature

The grander eighteenth-century owners planted trees on the periphery of their estates to shut out neighbouring houses, and had their parks remodelled to encompass lakes and woods, grassy glades, winding paths, romantic vistas and ha-has. They tried to create arcadias, to highlight nature, in direct contrast to the earlier seventeenth-century fashion, and the continuing European habit, of imposing formal

A Gothic summerhouse *nestling amongst a shaggy hedge of variegated greens, with grave-stones eccentrically propped against the bench inside. This is just the sort of understated idiosyncrasy which seasons the English landscape, whatever the county.*

Clusters of stone buildings *have unplanned symmetry as they huddle either side of the gateway leading to the stable yard beyond. There are interesting juxtapositions between the low wall to the right of the entranceway, crowned with wooden fencing, and the opposite wall, literally dripping with rock plants; between the two stone balls on the pair of gate posts, and the solitary ball in the right foreground. This relaxed haphazardness and the mellow gentleness exemplified, above right, by the E-shaped grouping of grey stone surmounted by a clock tower complete with bell, are definitive characteristics of British domestic architecture.*

terraces and parterres and long straight avenues upon the countryside, of constraining nature, rather than revelling in it.

For the upper and upper middle classes *were* revelling in it. They had reached a stage of sophistication where they could afford to react against their civilization and try to go back to nature, the wilder the better. Both the country and country pursuits became increasingly popular. Of course there were also pragmatic reasons for this. The first was the revolution in agriculture. The second, the improvement to roads and the speed of coaches. In the former case, landowners got caught up in the whole idea of land improvement. Although the aristocracy had farmed huge areas of their own land during the early Middle Ages, they had subsequently become more *rentiers* than working farmers, drawing rent from tenants and keeping perhaps just one farm to provide household provisions. They now began to farm large tracts of their land again, to plant more, drain and enclose and to encourage their tenants to make improvements also.

This new enthusiasm for the agrarian resulted in superior agricultural techniques, increased food output and doubled incomes. Given the success, it also kept landowners in the country for much longer periods.

Houses for balls and assemblies

The new and comparatively efficient network of roads made access to country houses very much easier and brought a good deal more sophistication to country dwellers as town gaieties and pleasures were introduced. Large mid-eighteenth-century country houses were specially designed for the kind of balls and assemblies that had previously been confined to London. No longer could landowners complain of boredom in the way that they often had before.

A Tudor brick gatehouse, *opposite, forms a striking mass, an imposing presence, in an otherwise gentle landscape. The arched gateway frames a long straight drive leading from the road to the grand gravel entrance to the house itself, glimpsed at the right of the picture. Gatehouses like this, of whatever period, are now being converted all over the British Isles to form dwellings themselves, albeit somewhat eccentric ones with their peculiarly narrow rooms and curiously shaped, haphazardly distributed windows.*

The nostalgic arched loggia *of this Victorian house looks as charming wreathed in the proverbial wraiths of mist as it does in the high sun. The wistaria-twisted arches frame arched murals painted on the walls inside, and the space makes, as it was intended to make, an ideal area for sheltered alfresco eating and lazy weekend lounging on the chaises.*

Sporting activities, which had been used hitherto more to pass the time than for pleasure, now became not just pleasing pastimes but positively virtuous, for along with the development of farms and farmland came an improvement in fox-hunting and shooting. Country gentlemen riding across country could feel at one with animals and nature, and simple communion with nature was becoming increasingly desirable. To walk or ride through unspoilt countryside, as Mark Girouard pointed out in his *Life in the English Country House,* seemed an enviable rather than a boring occupation. "Pictures of country houses no longer showed them thronged with people as had been the normal way of representing them up to this period, but appeared in idyllic solitude with perhaps just a single

Lazy games of croquet, *another ingredient of English country living, are played in numerous gardens all over the countryside. It somehow goes with the smell of new-mown grass, the sight of blue skies and roses; and just a glimpse of a pair of croquet mallets can give a frisson of pleasurable nostalgia for summer afternoons.*

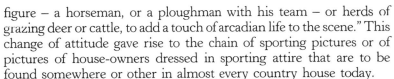

Glorified summerhouses *seem an essential part, somehow, of that famous British institution, the country house weekend. This one is exceptionally well-furnished for outdoor pleasures, with cane seats and cushions, coconut matting and curtains, as well as an unexpected but welcome fireplace against the none too rare times when summer weather is less than clement. Lead-paned windows and a beamed ceiling complete the Englishness.*

figure – a horseman, or a ploughman with his team – or herds of grazing deer or cattle, to add a touch of arcadian life to the scene." This change of attitude gave rise to the chain of sporting pictures or of pictures of house-owners dressed in sporting attire that are to be found somewhere or other in almost every country house today.

By the end of the eighteenth century, the English were inextricably entwining exteriors with interiors, not just by paying increased attention to the views from their windows, but by having long low-silled windows or French windows in ground-floor rooms opening straight out on to terraces or lawns. Rooms seemed to flow into gardens which flowed into the landscape, and by the same token, the gardens started flowing into the house with great pots and bouquets of

23

A conglomerate of styles *and bricks, new rooms added on over the generations, is very much a hallmark of rural British houses. Here, the house stands surrounded by parkland, the tall trees dwarfing an already tall building, their layered branches echoing the layered roof levels. The warm red brick abutting the grey makes a pleasing counterpoint to the long swards of green.*

A classically English country *setting: a sweep of green meadow strewn with early autumn leaves stretching beyond an old greystone manor house with its steeply pitched dark grey roofs and creepers growing up its mellowed walls.*

Pleasing juxtapositions are a dependable feature of English countryside. The somewhat formal lily pond with its central group of gambolling otters is an unexpected contrast to the tawny farmhouse with its charming white-painted Regency porch. But note how the house is beautifully and naturally framed by the tall trees on either side of the pond and the natural perspective that is formed by the stone surround leading up to the grassy walk through the curved beds of shrubs.

flowers filling the rooms, and eventually with conservatories overflowing with plants.

Houses for house parties

From this period to the end of the nineteenth century was the golden age of the large country house. Nature was no longer frightening or, worse, boring, but could be enjoyed to the hilt. It was comparatively easy, and generally very lucrative, to go on and on making improvements to house, contents and property. The solitude of the country was made all the more enjoyable by the knowledge that one could quickly get to London, or even to Europe, or alternatively fill the house with amusing people. If houses in the middle part of the eighteenth century had been designed for balls and assemblies, houses by the end of the century were being designed for house parties. The country house and its rural setting was fashioned as a conscious work of art to celebrate the pleasures of living.

Henry James remarked, "Of all the great things that the English have invented and made part of the credit of the national character, the most perfect, the most characteristic, the only one they have mastered completely in all its details so that it becomes a compendious illustration of their social genius and their manners, is the well-appointed, well-administered, well-filled country house."

A century later, the art critic Robert Hughes pointed out that neither English history nor English culture could be understood without understanding the collectively unique, historically indispensable phenomenon, the stately home. It matters far more as social evidence, he remarked, than most Italian palazzi or French chateaux. Certainly, in matters of taste, the English have never been purists like their European counterparts, and so much of the charm

White-painted garden seats *with elegant curved underpinnings are contrasted with the solidity of Versailles boxes on the other side of the lily pond pictured opposite. Again, this kind of formal grouping forms a pleasant composition with the fallen leaves, the reflections in the water and the softness of the lily pads surrounding the group of sculpted otters.*

Cobbled stable yards *are a familiar item in the long list of English country appurtenances. Here, cobblestones pave the entranceway and the brightly striped horse blanket positively glows against the background of variegated ochre stone and pleasantly arched windows. Note how the green-painted gutter beneath the tiled roof echoes the green fields outside the arched entrance.*

and character of so many country houses lies in layer upon layer of different styles, and in the contributions of so many different generations to the same rooms. Also, the sense of continuity and of oneness with the countryside is more in evidence in England than in Europe.

The historical French and Italian preference for living in the capital city with excursions to one's country estate, when either the heat or some unpleasantness at court made this desirable, is well-known. And in this century, European families under economic duress have mostly preferred to give up their country houses or villas rather than sell their homes in Paris or Rome, whereas the British in similar circumstances have invariably given up their London houses in order to retain the country homes at all costs and in any discomfort.

Old prams, dogs and rosy brick, *opposite, are as naturally elements of English country life as the mixture of climbing roses and tangled creepers on the walls, and the clumps of grey-green plants set against the stone pillar and paving in the middle of the drive.*

English eclecticism

Many people think of English country style in terms of those great houses, the stately homes which diminish little by little, whose eclectic and gracefully faded interiors are so emulated. But thanks to the prodigious desire for country life in the eighteenth and nineteenth centuries and the equally prodigious amount of building to satisfy the demand, the British Isles are full of other smaller country houses, manor houses and lodges, rectories and farms, village houses and cottages and *cottages ornés* which all bear the same rural stamp in lesser, but none the less beguiling, ways.

The British have rarely been serious visual creators but they are superb regurgitators, taking elements from the past and from other countries, sifting through classical and European architectural styles, adding fine collections of marbles or paintings, furniture or rugs, and generally finishing up with something essentially their own. But they have rarely reverenced the past as they do today. The great classics of the sixteenth, seventeenth, eighteenth and nineteenth centuries which are so lovingly cared for now were brilliantly new in their day. Earlier generations, though with the same magpie instincts as today, often got rid of a lot of the old in order to add their own contributions to a family house, and they were excited by adding on, rebuilding or building from scratch.

Today everything goes

Interestingly, today's buyers, who glory in rescuing much of what their forbears despised, or used for the servants, and whose houses are full of scrubbed old oak or pine, shapeless, comfortable sofas, William Morris fabrics or revival chintzes, blazing log fires and huge bowls of tumbling leaves, are propounding what they think of as traditional English country style. Nevertheless, they are still producing something endemic to this century, just as the late decorator John Fowler,

Ancient barns are a familiar feature, but few are so well-accoutred as this one, pictured opposite above, with its massive beamed roof, its flagstoned floor, the old grinding wheel and the cache of agricultural implements. But it also acts as a storage area for odd pieces of furniture: an oak settle, a table, a frail blue-painted wheelchair. The most interesting feature, of course, is the contrast of the stained glass window by Frank Avray Wilson and the straw-fringed stone, the ancient timber and the sunny, shaggy fields outside.

A handsome brace of pheasants *hung against the stone wall of a barn is as much a part of a British winter as the sight of a shooting party clumping through a ploughed field, or dogs leaping through hedges in search of fallen game. Look at the variegated tawny colours of the stone and its lovely irregularity.*

Sweet, English lavender *is part of the fabric of many English houses, whether grown outside in beds bordering the house or garden, or tucked away in drawers and closets to scent clothes and linen. Here, a mixture of naturally dried and fresh stems lies waiting in a trug to be dispersed indoors.*

Gardens of benign neglect *are certainly an integral part of the country, as much by choice as by circumstance. Then too, the English love vignettes and long views, groupings at the ends of walks or paths. White-painted chairs look well against warm brick walls, which in turn look good against grassy flagstones, overhanging branches, mossy lawns and meandering flower borders beside typically uneven paths.*

whose inspiration was the eighteenth and early nineteenth century, and whose knowledge of their decorating and window treatment techniques was immense, always created something that was essentially John Fowler rather than a recreation of an earlier period. The common denominator is the framework of the English countryside itself, or its influence.

With English country style it is not so much that anything goes, as it is the art of making sure that everything does go, and goes harmoniously; that nothing jars, nothing stands out too obtrusively. William Thackeray, writing in an early *Punch,* summed up an ideal country weekend: "Air fragrant with a large bouquet on the writing table, the linen fragrant with the lavender in which it had been laid . . . all flowers and freshness, all peace, plenty, happiness". He could have added, it is waking up to the cooing of wood pigeons, the crowing of the cock, the waft of sweet, unsullied air through open windows. It is above all a kind of comfort of the senses and of peace: elusive elements which are perhaps the key to an ideal English country style.

CHAPTER TWO

HALLS LANDINGS & STAIRCASES

Those delicious old houses, in the long August days . . .
HENRY JAMES writing in 1876

From parrot cage *to barometer,*
the hall opposite betrays the
generally eclectic attitude of the
English. With its many doors
opening off to numerous other
rooms, its uncompromising table
in the middle of the floor with its
visitors' book at the ready, and its
practical stone floor, this hall is a
vestibule rather than a living
space, the hub for the rest of the
house. Note the old bells that were
so much a feature of houses with a
large staff to summon.

f all rooms, the hall has the longest pedigree in
English decoration. Up until the fourteenth
century it was the chief room in any dwelling in
Britain, sometimes the only room, and many
large country houses in Britain are given the
epithet of hall as a result. This medieval space was
a very long cry from the entrance hall of today,
however spacious, although the conventional decoration of arms,
shields and hunting trophies that bedeck so many contemporary halls
dates back to the needs of the Middle Ages.

Medieval halls

The word "manor", one of the generic words for a large English
country house, was introduced into the English language after the
Norman Conquest in 1066 and came from the French *manoir*, a
dwelling, although it ended up meaning the whole estate of a lord.
Manor houses in early Norman England consisted of the main hall and

A two-storeyed Norman hall
still standing in the grounds of a
later house in Lincolnshire.

Handsome, curving staircases *were a feature of eighteenth- and nineteenth-century houses. Both spaces shown here pay respect to the traditional ingredients and proportions but with an eye to twentieth-century lightness – and use of light. Note the traditional wall lights and table lamps backed by recessed ceiling spots in the pale terracotta hall. (The method of painting is described in chapter 9.) Clear yellow paint, freshened with sparkling white woodwork and a light marble floor, enhances a natural airiness.*

a few outbuildings grouped around a courtyard. In big houses, the room was always aisled because at that time it was technically impossible to roof a wide span. Early halls looked therefore rather like churches – on which they were modelled – with a narrow but lofty nave flanked by wide, corridor-like spaces edged with wooden posts or stone pillars which supported separate sloping roofs. These side spaces were usually used for storage or for housing the servants.

The outside door, or doors, situated on the long walls were generally shielded from the weather by a porch, sometimes as elaborately carved as the porch of a church. And there was always a central hearth with smoke curling up from the fire through a draughty hole in the roof, until, in the thirteenth century, the hole was fitted with a pottery louvre like a primitive chimney, though it looked more like a beehive. Wood screens were set on both sides of the door to stop smoke blowing everywhere every time the door was opened, and eventually these screens evolved into a continuous structure or inner wall with doors leading into the main space so that they formed a long corridor

Wide, wooden stairs *and carved banisters were an impressive part of Tudor and Jacobean houses, frequently copied by the Victorians. The stairway pictured opposite has many traditional elements: elaborately pelmeted curtains at the long windows; polished, uncarpeted treads; a large and ancient tapestry; early portraits; and, of course, vases of fresh flowers on the windowsills. Decoration is kept to a minimum so that the elements of the house – the distinguished woodwork and the graceful windows – are shown to advantage, as is the green countryside through the glass.*

A high Victorian hall *complete with arched doorway and deep lincrustered dado leads into a Turkish-carpeted dining room which leads in turn to a splendid balustraded terrace, a true nineteenth-century delight. The leather couch is draped with skins and the proverbial marbled hall floor is in fact vinyl tiles. The mirror looks as if it was an original overmantel above a fireplace.*

known as the "screens passage". These screens were often made of linenfold panelling which was sometimes embellished with brilliantly coloured painting.

At the far end of the hall was a dais where the family ate – at the high table so to speak – while the rest of the household and retainers sat on benches at trestle tables below. The walls around the dais would be either panelled with wainscoting or hung with tapestries or cheaper painted cloths, and sometimes there would be a painting on the wall above. Tapestries might line other parts of the hall too if the owner was particularly prosperous, or there might be more painted cloths.

Arms and armour were always in evidence so that a constant check could be kept on their whereabouts, and the walls were also hung with heraldic shields and crested helmets belonging to the landlord and his band of knights or squires. Coats of arms were often painted on walls and later incorporated into stained glass in the ubiquitous oriel windows of the sixteenth century. Later too, a land-owner might insert rows of heraldic shields into the panelling of his

Dark oak stairs *are much too nice to be carpeted. Left like this their age and patina can be appreciated. Leaded window panes make intensely strong patterns on the wall in the bright sunlight and are shielded at night by short green and white cotton curtains, which reflect the deep green of the garden outside – glimpsed near the bottom of the stairs.*

A narrow oak staircase shielded by a door, heavy brace beams, a nice old brick floor, and a mixture of painted brick and boarding on the walls are all typical ingredients of an old cottage hallway. Brick floors like these were a great improvement on the former beaten earth and were often used when flags were not available or proved too expensive. They are also highly practical for country entranceways, withstanding the worst scourges of muddy feet and paws. Old bricks can be found in builders' yards and on demolition sites, and even new bricks can be made to look satisfactorily beaten up if maltreated (see chapter 9). The handsome turned oak chair is a solid foil to the cluster of rosettes gained over many years from gymkhanas and horse shows.

screen wall, representing the different marriage alliances of his family over the generations, and this obsession with heraldic motifs that were originally designed to show off a family's influence and distinction has threaded its colourful way through centuries of different halls, just as one will still see old arms, guns and hunting trophies.

The worst thing about medieval halls, which happily has had no influence on current decoration, was the floors, often referred to as the "marsh" and with good reason. They were usually of beaten earth, although a few grander houses had a stone base, and they were littered with straw, rushes, bones, scraps and general filth and were another good reason for the raised dais for the lords and masters. On a visit to England as late as the fifteenth century Erasmus was shocked by English floors and described them as "commonly of clay, strewed with rushes under which lie unmolested an ancient collection of beer, grease, fragments, bones, spittle, excrements of dogs and cats and everything that is nasty". All too often the habit was to throw a new layer of rushes on top of the old rather than clear the litter.

The glorious proportions *of the eighteenth century are shown to particular advantage in this graceful hall with its equally graceful forecourt beyond the open door. The long, arched windows with their deep window seats need no covering; indeed, any sort of window treatment would have only hidden their delicacy. The marble squares on the floor need no rugs. The panelling has been subtly painted and coloured (see chapter 9). Furniture has been kept to an elegant minimum, as have prints and accessories, which mainly consist of plants and the ever-useful barometer. The main point is the gentle harmony of proportion, colour and view. Nothing jars, nothing stands out, but every component conspires towards a thoroughly pleasing impression.*

Collections of hats *piled
irreverently on classical busts or
phrenologists' heads are a fairly
frequent sight in English halls. It
is a custom both lighthearted and
practical, as it turns out. After all,
hats are both decorative and quite
hard to store . . . . In this case, the
somewhat eclectic pile of headgear
nicely fills the arched niche, as
well as relieving the space from too
much classical allusion.*

A deep panelled dado *is a nineteenth-century characteristic. In the picture opposite it is combined with wallpaper designed by Pugin for the House of Lords as the background for another spacious living hall that is very much a twentieth-century living room. The heavily ornamented plaster ceiling is offset by the simplicity of the coia matting, and the lighting, which does not make any pretension to particular aesthetics, will throw light where it is needed: for anyone reading on the chair or sofa by the fire; or for someone writing at the sofa table. A second writing table is used for books, magazines and pot pourri; and family portraits are lined on the walls.*

Comfortable "living" halls *were very much a feature of grand houses in the nineteenth century. This one, with its heavily carved panelling and decorated ceiling, its fireplace and positive plethora of comfortable, chintz-covered armchairs and skirted lamp tables piled with books, is a splendid example of the genre. The well-furnished writing table in the foreground, the club fender at the fireplace, the mellowness of the blending red and white fabric, carpet and oriental rug all combine in a comforting opulence.*

For several centuries the hall continued to be the place for dining, drinking, carousing, listening to music, community meetings, law courts (called "the Moot", hence the Moot Halls in English villages, and the moot points in an argument) and for sleeping around the fire. Little changed. Sometimes in the fifteenth century a gallery was built over the screens passage for musicians and minstrels. The fireplace moved from its central position to the wall and gained a cylindrical chimney and a pyramidal hood. The only substantial change came with the advent of the "solar" – again derived from the French *soler*, an upstairs room. This provided private apartments for the family reached by primitive steps of wood or stone in a corner of the hall. The move was resented by the populace. It was a move away from the communality of medieval life and this was never restored.

Elizabethan halls
The servants ate on in the great hall until Elizabethan times when they moved with the kitchens below stairs, but the hall remained impres-

Dogs proliferate, *whether of painted stone on a granite base or the real shaggy thing, and both contrast nicely with the faux stone walls, the stone floors and the monochromatic colour scheme. A harness flung casually over the stone dog happens to repeat the lines of the iron candlestick on the wall above, and the delicate rays of pale sun superimpose their own faint pattern on the pinky beige of the prevailing colouring.*

sive for it was meant to impress. It lost its dais because this was no longer necessary, but it was still the entry point for visitors as well as the formal starting point for the great processions of food to the new separate eating place which became common at this time. In great country houses there was often now an elaborate gallery used both for musicians and as a sort of inspection post for checking on the household doings below. Plaster ceilings, often very elaborate with geometric patterns of squares and octagons or "frets", were installed below the ceiling joists. With the advent of the proper staircase, as opposed to the narrow wood or stone steps of the medieval years, woodcarving reached equally splendid heights of elaboration.

Palladian and neo-Palladian

Once houses started to be built on two storeys and the kitchen relegated to the basement, the entrance hall began to be more of a vestibule and less of a living space, especially when the staircase began to be incorporated, for it was often very wide and splendid. In the eighteenth century, however, in the grand houses most important rooms including the main bedrooms were brought down to the ground floor again, following the tentative introduction of first the Palladian style by Inigo Jones in the 1660s, and then, nearly a hundred years later, the neo-Palladian introduced by the great amateur architect Lord Burlington. In such houses, halls became very splendid again, to conform to the Palladian–Burlington rules of "harmonic proportions".

"A hall", wrote Isaac Ware in *The Complete Book of Architecture* (1756), "must be large and noble since it serves as Summer room for dining; it is an ante-chamber in which people of business or of the second rank wait and amuse themselves, and it is a good apartment for the reception of large companies at public feasts."

A splendid fanlight *backs an imposing pillared entrance in an eighteenth-century hallway, opposite, and together they frame the kind of lovely, lengthy green view that is meant to refresh the jaded soul. And there are some very pleasing juxtapositions: the elaborate cornice with the* trompe l'oeil *stone walls; the elegant lanterns with the sturdy flagged floor; the simple door to the left with the grandeur and double doors of the main entrance; the reflective profiles of stone and live dogs; and the piles of firewood outside on the step with the sturdy green leaves on the stone plinth. Everything looks strong and practical but also graceful.*

The magnificent carvings and woodwork of the Elizabethan period, particularly on staircases, the splendour of the Baroque, gave way to marble and stone and much more sombre colouring. Most halls still had fireplaces with blazing fires in the winter, which was just as well given the damp British cold. The classical busts, statuary, fragments of ruins and other oddities that gentlemen on the grand tour brought back from their travels, culled from archaeological remains or from the great Italian collections then being sold, were considered more appropriate decoration than paintings. However, in lesser houses, belonging to lesser country gentlemen, yeomen and farmers, owners began to hang sporting paintings and prints.

Neo-Classicism
Adam and the fashion for neo-Classicism are responsible for some of the most beautiful halls in existence, although Vanbrugh's glorious Baroque wonder at Castle Howard in Yorkshire (seen to such effect as Brideshead in the television adaptation of Waugh's *Brideshead Re-*

A particularly good example *of clear, graphic stencilling is shown here, with the design used as a graceful border under the cornice and around the fireplace. The colours look fresh and clear against their stippled background and the matting on the floor, and look good, too, against the white-painted Victorian fireplace and the woodwork. Such borders certainly enliven any wall, and can also be used on floors and furniture (see chapter 9).*

A dining hall *that has a particularly graphic quality, provided as much by the hanging of the unusual black and white prints against the strong blue of the walls as by the distinctive horizontal lines made by the white chair rail and deep skirting or base-boards. The furniture too stands out with unusual clarity against such a background. The flat basket full of lavender and the bowl of pot pourri add softening touches, as does the wall candelabra.*

visited) is spectacular, as is the Palladian stone hall by Colen Campbell and William Kent at Houghton Hall in Norfolk. Adam and his disciples used marble for splendid fluted and carved columns and friezes as well as for exquisite floors, chimneypieces and overmantels. Ceilings were exceedingly ornamental with delicate plasterwork and colouring: roses, pale greens, sky blues and honey beiges. By contrast some of Adam's floors were executed in rich colours like reds and ochres, umbers and blue-greys.

Nostalgia in the nineteenth century
During the late eighteenth and early nineteenth centuries the medieval theme of weapons, shields and helmets was often translated into plaster reliefs, pastiches of the real thing, variations on a theme, just as classical symbols like columns and fragments of ruins are part

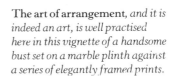

The art of arrangement, *and it is indeed an art, is well practised here in this vignette of a handsome bust set on a marble plinth against a series of elegantly framed prints.*

The graphic quality *of the dining hall pictured opposite extends to the handsome silver cup full of airy dried seed pods, to the silver, the cut glass and the mahogany sideboard. The clear blue walls are an object lesson in the use of strong colour to display objets d'art.*

of the shorthand used by the contemporary Post-Modernists. Equally, although in a considerably less restrained manner, the romance of the Middle Ages was being recreated with collections of real (and reproduction) arms and armour in the new craze for the "Gothick". The nineteenth-century hall was a monument to nostalgia – all sorts of nostalgia – with neo-Norman, neo-Elizabethan and, of course, neo-Gothic interiors appearing everywhere as well as the earlier established neo-Classical.

Traditional beamed white walls *of battered plaster make a comely background for a pair of exquisitely worked flintlocks and a collection of old seascapes. In medieval times the weapons hanging in the hall were there for instant readiness as well as for a display of power. Here, they are on display for the beauty of their inlay and for the rarity of their workmanship. The simplicity of the picture frames contrasts well with the intricately inlaid stocks and the dark irregularity of the old oak beams.*

An old farmhouse hall, *opposite, provides a sturdy, timeless background for an arresting family portrait. In many rooms, the picture's size would have dwarfed all surrounding objects, but the thick walls, the simplicity, and the warm glow of the colour wash and of the stripped wood floor (see chapter 9) allow for a good deal of idiosyncrasy in the way of objects and pictures. The space is both utilitarian and, in its own way, elegant, for there is a certain insouciant grandeur in the juxtaposition of heavy gilt frames with plaster, of simple country door with nice solid nineteenth-century chairs. The longcase, or grandfather, clock is almost as familiar a sight in English halls as the ubiquitous dogs and wellington boots.*

In "The Princess" (1847), Lord Tennyson describes the somewhat catholic hall of a pure neo-Classical house:
". . . showed the house
Greek, set with busts: from vases in the hall
Flowers of all heavens, and lovelier than their names,
Grew side by side, and on the pavement lay
Carved stones of the Abbey ruin in the park,
Huge Ammonites and the first bones of time.
And on the tables every clime and age
Jumbled together; celts and calumets,
Claymore and snowshoe, toys in lava, fans
Of sandal, amber, ancient rosaries,
Laborious orient ivory sphere in sphere,
The cursed Malaysian crease and battle clubs
From the Isles of Palm. And higher on the walls
Betwixt the monstrous horns of elk and deer,
His own forefather's arms and armour hang."

The modern ideal

The vision that many people now have of an English country hall is not so very far removed from Tennyson's mid-nineteenth-century description with its collection of peculiar objects, profusion of flowers, antlers, arms and armour. The former may well be more domestic, more nostalgic, more *comfortable*, but one senses the same curious mixture of "things enchanting and extraordinary", as Thomas Hope wrote in his *Household Furniture and Interior Decoration* (1807), the same eclecticism that is forever England.

So what are the components of the ideal English country hall today? The contemporary version would include a great many of the

A grouping of pewter plates *together with a shelf full of assorted jugs and other pewter items adds interest to an alcove wall in a back hall. The jugs are lit from behind by an architectural strip light, and stippling (see chapter 9) gives a special glow to the walls.*

ingredients of the past. There would, for example, almost certainly be a flickering fire of some sweet-scented wood like apple, fed by logs piled into baskets of woven rush, or wooden trugs, or a battered hamper. To the side of the staircase there might be an old carved chest or massive table with great jugs of leaves or flowers, bowls of *pot pourri*, a mixture of casually flung magazines, letters, tweed hats and caps and odd gardening gloves.

Floors, walls and firelight
The floor will be of flagstones, or waxed brick, or polished floor boards, or coia matting, or, in grander houses, marble, and there will probably be an oriental rug or two or a couple of bright Kelims. Walls

A miscellaneous collection *of hats from different eras, and from a variety of travels and colonial postings adorns a mahogany bench against a panelled dado. Along with the contemporary riding boots, still in use, they offer a little potted family history all their own.*

A converted farmhouse in the West country has an agreeably relaxed living hall with a comfortable mix of casual armchairs and a sofa (in foreground) set around the fire, an oriental rug on a tiled floor, generous bunches of flowers, logs in a rush basket, cushions and a dog, supplemented on this occasion by a cat. Judiciously placed reading lights cast a pleasant glow on the fireplace wall. The deeply embrasured window has a solid wooden shutter, in harmony with the banisters on the other side of the fire.

will be beamed, or panelled, or wainscoted or dadoed, or hung with tapestries, and if there is any spare bit of wall not painted white, it will be marbled or distressed in some way or painted a faux stone or covered in gently-patterned paper above a dado rail, or painted a warm terracotta, apricot, yellow or rose as a contrast to the more inclement periods of English weather.

Actually, the bad reputation of English weather is something of an anomaly when it comes face to face with the more nostalgic vision of country living, for when the proverbial sweet-smelling fire is not throwing dancing shadows around, there are invariably equally pro-verbial shafts of sunlight gilding the faded mahogany or casting pools of golden light on to the oak, or making the gilt of the picture frames gleam. But then, flickering firelight and the endless subtle changes in the quality of daylight are two of the constant factors of English country life, and the interiors are inevitably shaped by them. Almost every major room in any kind of English country house has a fireplace, and windows are positioned to let in every last glimmer of light.

An efficient wood-burning stove has ousted the handsome fireback from this old cottage fireplace. The room was formerly a sitting room, but with various additions to the original structure it has now become a comfortable sitting-hall. The fine collection of old Bristol glass is virtually framed by two old guns – the long and the short of it, for the top one is a blunderbuss and the other an exceptionally long flintlock.

Pictures and objects

Other components are more variable but none the less predictable. There may well be, for example, sporting prints of one kind and another, especially up the stairs, and sporting trophies, or at least hunting, shooting and fishing trophies, and mementoes of martial and other past glories. Or there might be handsome architectural prints, or political cartoons, or old maps of the relevant county, or pleasant landscapes or family portraits. There will certainly be a mirror, and maybe a longcase or grandfather clock, or perhaps some of those quirks of fancy that the English are prone to: an overlong, longcase clock crammed into a well dug out of a corner of a brick floor, as I once actually saw in a low-ceilinged cottage hall; a plaster bust used as a hat stand; a pair of stone sleeping dogs flanked by somnolent real ones; pairs of old shoe lasts marching up the treads of a narrow cottage staircase.

Depending on the rurality and formality of the house, there will be stands full of golf umbrellas and shooting sticks, old tennis racquets or

The Cotswold stone of this old chimneybreast has been plastered over to leave just the original opening and surround. The nicely battered flagstone floor has been left untouched and forms a subtle contrast with the dazzling white of the walls. Following centuries of tradition, the fireplace, when not in use, is filled with green boughs and bunches of fresh bright leaves.

The unselfconscious haphazard *style of decorating common in the twentieth century from 1918 onwards is applied to the room here. This is definitely not a living hall – although it could be. Just add a club fender to the fireplace, a couple of armchairs or a sofa, or both, perhaps a window seat in the deep embrasure, uplights to the corners, and a reading light or two, and the ambience would be changed without detracting from the pleasantly laid-back look.*

Handsome juxtapositions *of objects whether different in shape or subject form the compositions, the small vignettes, that make a house memorable. Clustered on shelves, windowsills, table-tops, mantelshelves, they are the arrangements that give life and substance to a room. Here, a Chinese vase in front of a splendid platter is caught in a white shaft of sunlight.*

The elegant formality *of the beautifully proportioned hall pictured opposite is offset by whimsey and a precise sense of scale and colour. Generous side tables with baskets of logs underneath are formed by resting creamy rectangular tops on appropriate lengths of tree trunk. Groups of prints are meticulously hung in tiers, and the many-hatted Roman busts look good under the ginger jars.*

the odd adolescent cricket bat, and rows of shooting, wellington and riding boots, although these might well be relegated to the back hall if there is one. These back halls are invariably highly practical. Floors will certainly by stone-flagged or quarry-tiled or covered with old pamments to minimize the havoc caused by muddy boots and paws, and walls will usually be serviceably painted rather than "decorated". Any wall ornamentation will usually be confined to school or university group photographs, old shooting or fishing photographs and records, stuffed fish or birds, oars, things in glass domes, and colonial memorabilia if there was any sort of colonial past. Alternatively, there may just be rows of pegs for coats, old jackets, hats and huskies – those quilted jackets and vests so popular with the English. And scattered

Unusual pieces of furniture *often find their ways into halls, where they can be both admired in passing for their aesthetic or flamboyant qualities and at the same time act as useful receptacles for the clutter and memorabilia that invariably collect. The carved green-rubbed cupboard contrasts well with the blue woven rug; the painted dresser is a splendid repository for family memorabilia.*

Old boots, old hats, *coats, raincoats, stuff you do not want to throw away but don't know what to do with, all crammed into a closet or cupboard, are a familiar sight in any back hall. These muddy wellingtons and haphazardly fallen felt hat are, in their way, as much a part of integral decoration as any thought-up scheme, for back halls usually just happen in the natural course of things.*

Agreeable juxtapositions, *left, of sophisticated painting on plain plastered wall, riding hats and crop with early oak furniture, and fine Samarkand rug on coia matting. The still-life this presents betrays an owner of civilized tastes and an aesthetic understanding.*

A well-used hall *is comfortable to enter and leave. The one pictured opposite, with its military umbrella stands crammed with shooting-sticks, riding crops, riding hats, walking sticks and canes, along with the mahogany boots stand and the boots themselves, instantly proclaims the equine interests of its owners. The velvet curtain, serving as a draught-excluder, and the oriental rug visually soften the hardness of the old flagstones, their polished finish differentiating them from similar stones outside. And for some unfathomable, yet I am sure interesting, reason, preserved turtles seem to be almost as ubiquitous in English hallways as living dogs. Anyway, they look well on the flagstones.*

around will be dog baskets, riding hats, crops, whips, gun racks, fishing tackle, even saddles and bridles, and somewhere an old table for gardening gloves, secateurs and trowels ready for the quick prune or weed – all part and parcel of the British outdoor life.

In Edwardian or turn-of-the-century houses (whose opulent comfort has been added to the elegant legacy of the eighteenth century in most people's ideas of English style) front halls might have stained glass windows with heraldic devices, or rows of colourful coats of arms on shields propped up above the picture rail in tune with the recurrent nostalgia for the medieval. In any type of house, especially on landing spaces, there might be slightly ramshackle bookshelves crammed with the wildest miscellany of books from Arthur Ransome to family medicine. These shelves may be wedged along turns in the stairs, along corridors, or line the wider spaces between stairways in taller houses. Such landing spaces might also boast a table or chest, plants, oriental vases, or in some cases they might even be given a desk and chair if there is room.

Beautiful, gleaming furniture *in a traditional setting is one of the obvious delights of an old English country house. Here, the grouping of exquisite marquetry chairs with the most elegant spinet and its spare grouping of clock and jars is a reassuring reminder that the sun has still not quite set over the Empire.*

Lighting: authentic and practical

Lighting, in this hybrid example of an English country hall, would almost certainly be from at least a couple of ceiling-hung Georgian or nineteenth-century glass lanterns, boosted by either wall lights or the occasional table lamp. In grander houses, especially houses with wide and sweeping staircases, there would be a chandelier of some size, with dim brass picture lights centred over any paintings. Since, however, electricity is somewhat *parvenu*, and the romantic view of an English country hall implies the sort of mellowness provided by candlelight, or, at the very latest, oil or gas, bear in mind that just such a feeling of mellow warmth can be achieved by using the best of the traditional lighting fixtures, enhanced with judiciously placed uplights set in corners and behind furniture. These bounce a subtle light upwards, and should be controlled, as indeed should all the light fixtures, by a dimmer switch. Possessions, depending upon their positioning, can then be highlighted by spots or wallwashers (in the case of a wall of prints, for example). For safety's sake, the treads and risers of wood or stone stairs should be lit either by positioning wall lights up the staircase walls with light focussing downwards, or by siting downlights to provide the best practical light. With really good subtle lighting one barely notices the actual fixtures, so it can be used to enhance the most ancient setting or the most cottagey of cottages with impunity.

Curtains

There is no real need for curtains or window coverings in a country hall, unless they are to make the place seem warmer or cosier at night, in which case any large window might have looped-back curtains or draperies to be released or restrained by tie-backs at will. If small

A Regency rent table, *opposite, fits comfortably into the curve of the staircase, as well as offsetting the tall vertical lines of the traditional longcase clock. The rag-rubbed terracotta walls (see chapter 9) look well against the flagstone floor, the handsome furniture and the mahogany staircase. Siting a table lamp in such a position adds to the general sense of warmth.*

Windowsills are nice places *for displaying almost anything. Here a glass jar of flowers catches the sun and makes an agreeable composition with the stone sill and the thick white walls.*

Back halls and narrow stairs *are not usually glittering examples of decoration to emulate, but they are very much a part of any English house of size, and have a nodding familiarity with many a basement floor in early town houses as well. This is a good example of just such an unforced look, and agreeable with its row of room bells for the servants, its nice old timepiece, the blue and white serving platters, the bleached boards and painted staircase, the old scullery beyond, and even the bicycle.*

Windows do not need dressing *of any sort when, like this, they are deeply set in a thick wall with a gentle garden view beyond. Indeed, uncluttered in this way, they seem more like a painting, and need only an object on the sill: a plant, a single-stem vase, a jug, perhaps, or a bowl, or, as here, a nicely painted container of* pot pourri. *The gently rag-rubbed walls (see chapter 9) and radiator, and the distressed window frame throw the view from the window into conspicuous relief.*

Lace curtains *at the window give a softening effect here, and the centre panel of the shutters is subtly emphasized by the painted lattice design, which picks up the green of the walls (outside the picture). Note the brass tie-back which restrains the folds of the lace so competently.*

windows have good sills, they are ideal for collections of glass, an old jug, or some Victorian or Edwardian object in a domed glass case.

Furniture

Furniture depends almost entirely upon the size of the hall. Larger rooms might have a pair of armchairs, or an old couch or chesterfield, and possibly a library-cum-dining table as well for occasional or regular dining. Even cottage halls, which are normally miniscule, will have some sort of side table and chair, or possibly an old bench and some idiosyncratic possessions.

No one hall would have all the components mentioned, but it would have some of them, proving that the English country style of today is a comfortable and comforting amalgam, layered with memories and traditions whose roots have mainly been forgotten or only half-recollected. The point is that the hall should be a pleasant place through which to enter a house and a pleasant place to leave from, and that has been the case for centuries.

CHAPTER THREE

SITTING ROOMS

*. . . our Englishman, mindful of fireside joys, of capacious
easy chairs . . .*
Paris 1925, THE ARCHITECTURAL REVIEW

A nicely eclectic *country room,
opposite, in a charmingly updated
farmhouse. Warm, cluttered,
cosy, ebullient, colourful, complete
with low-slung beams and uneven
floors, it is the very model of the
eclectic English country style.
Looked at carefully, it defies most
careful decorating codes. Nothing
particularly "goes" with anything
else, at least not in the
conventional sense, yet all the
elements cohere into a harmonious
whole without looking in the least
calculated, including the harp and
piano in the far corner.*

The comfortable, easy look of the English country sitting room has been one of Britain's biggest invisible exports since the late nineteenth century. It has been so emulated and admired that one tends to forget that the English did not really think much about comfort in decoration until the Regency period, in spite of Francis Bacon's seventeenth-century stricture that "houses are built to live in, and not to look on. Therefore let use bee preferred before uniformitie, except where both may bee had." As John Cornforth points out in his *English Interiors 1790-1848*, the English country house style with its lived-in look owes a great deal to the decorational approach of people in the period 1825-45, "who set out to create a sense of informality and ease through a synthesis of furniture of different dates and styles with deliberate contrasts between relaxing chairs and sofas and furniture that may be more formal and grand in design and attention."

A squashy, comforting sofa *in a
simple striped cotton is teamed
with a mixture of chintz and
embroidered cushions or pillows.
The dégagé but felicitous mixture
with its strongly personal note is
typical of the kind of rural style
where comfort is – as it should be –
much more important than
careful coordination.*

67

More comfortable pillows *or cushions on the Englishman's proverbial armchair, but this time in the elaborate* petit-point *so beloved of many Englishwomen.*

East meets West *or, more accurately, the English countryside in this mellow room with its oriental landscapes and embroidered silks arranged around the old brick fireplace. It is a nice mix, along with the tweed sofas and embroidered pillows or cushions, and the small bits of silver that contrast with the lusty brown pottery lamp base, the whole enhanced by the sunlight shafting across the blazing firelight.*

English eclecticism

Comfort might not have been a principal ingredient of English style before the nineteenth century but eclecticism was. Rooms in more ordinary English country houses rarely started out with any particularly coherent character, nor indeed did grander ones unless they happened to be designed by some great landmark architect like Vanbrugh, William Kent, Colen Campbell, Robert Adam or James Wyatt, and were therefore deeply prized and preserved.

By far the greater majority changed gradually as new fashions followed old and owners added this or that detail to an already existing decoration. For then, as now, the mass of people rarely changed a room from top to bottom. Just as the English added piecemeal to the exterior of a house over the years, so they added piecemeal to a room and its contents. For example, a nineteenth-century watercolour (circa 1840) of the drawing room at Aldenham Park, the family home of the Actons, shows it to be divided by Tudor arches, to possess a neo-Classical ceiling with two "Victory" candelabra from a previous

Regency makeover, and every conceivable style of chair and table.

That arbiter of early nineteenth-century taste, Thomas Hope, wrote his *Household Furniture and Interior Decoration* (1807) as the British equivalent of the book *Recueils de Décorations Intérieures* (1808) by the great architects of the Napoleonic era, Percier and Fontaine. "While the French are beginning to make the most rapid strides towards the purest style of the antique," he admonished, "shall we obstinately lag behind because of an irrational adherence to a vitiated and corrupt style?" He was referring to the picturesque style popular at the period, but he himself did not entirely keep to the Greek and Egyptian revival which he advocated so ardently. A Miss Mitford, visiting Rosedale Cottage, one of Hope's country residences, observed: "The Saloon Chinese, full of jars and Mandarins and Pagodas; the library Egyptian, all covered with hieroglyphics and swarming with furniture, crocodiles and sphinxes. Only think of a crocodile couch and a sphinx sofa! They sleep in Turkish tents and dine in a Gothic chapel."

Sumptuous gilded leather *and inlaid marquetry, nineteenth-century furniture mixed with seventeenth-century, nice old tawny velvet cushions on a battered, deeply comfortable 1930s leather couch are all put together in this modern addition to a seventeenth-century cottage. An impressive seventeenth-century portrait and an elegant longcase clock dominate the room.*

69

Four uncoordinated prints, *a complicated oriental carpet, an embroidered stool and a heavily decorated oriental panelled screen subside gently into each other in an eminently comfortable rural sitting room. The massive, simple stone fireplace and white-painted beams, and the several light sources make a calm framework for the use of pattern on pattern on pattern. . . .*

Hope's taste was clearly very far from that cosiness so endemic to English country style today. The novelist, Maria Edgeworth, visiting another of Hope's houses, Deepdene in Surrey, wrote: "This house is magnificently furnished – but to my taste, much too fine for a country house, even making the idea of comfort improbable."

The withdrawing room

In fact the sitting room, or withdrawing room, did not really come into existence until the reign of Elizabeth I. Its origin lay in the "solar", the first room to be built as an adjunct to the medieval great hall. By Elizabethan times, most large houses had a "great chamber" for receptions. This was rather architectural and masculine in feeling, in

contrast to the more feminine, more familial withdrawing room. The great chambers or saloons were used at first for eating as well as for receiving guests and were arranged with sets of formal chairs and tables along the sides of the room. The withdrawing room was primarily a place to retire to after meals, or for dining in private before the advent of the parlour.

Withdrawing room walls were first covered in tapestries or hangings, ranging from painted linens or plain wools or worsteds (available in a far wider variety than they are today) to the richest of silks, silk velvets and gilt leathers, so sumptuous that they had to be protected by overcloths when the rooms were not in use. Most hangings were made to fit a particular wall and, whether of silk, velvet, wool or

To misquote Gilbert and Sullivan, this is the very model of a major English drawing room with its wonderful mixture of prints, chintzes, damasks and silks, not to mention pattern on pattern. Yet the soft grey walls bind it altogether, as indeed do the plants and the crisp white woodwork.

71

Mixed leaves *from variegated plants tumble from shelf to shelf in this conservatory, the various greens beautifully caught in the shaft of sunlight.*

Exquisite Victorian copies *of stone-mullioned Elizabethan windows were actually found on a demolition site and installed in this harmonious room with its gentle view over the pond and field to the woods beyond. With its serene furnishings and rugs, its books, music stand and piano (outside the picture), the space is imbued with the nineteenth-century spirit of the library cum family and general entertaining room, though in fact it is part of a converted barn brought from another county.*

73

Old patchwork quilts *make handsome tablecloths, as well as forming a gently coloured background for the collection of objects, flowers and porcelain on this occasional table. The roses on the lampshade are unself-consciously repeated with clusters of the real thing. Assemblies of unrelated objects are very English country style.*

A symphony of yellows *is created in the drawing room above, with its mixture of pattern against pattern set on ochre herringbone matting. The curtains are nicely finished off with a yellow trim and green-yellow cord tie-backs, and the skirts of the table draw back to reveal a television when needed.*

worsted, they were woven in considerably narrower widths (about 20-21 inches) than fabrics today. Seams were usually disguised by applied trimmings and there would often be a border around the room, again to hide frayed ends.

Window curtains stayed rather utilitarian until the end of the seventeenth century and were usually made of silk taffeta and liners which were pulled to one side or up rather than being divided in the middle. Tables were often covered with "carpets" made of fabrics matching the window curtains, or of some simpler stuff, or specially woven tapestry, embroidered linen or, indeed, carpet.

People who could afford the oriental carpets then being imported were sometimes sufficiently extravagant to lay them on the floor, but most displayed smaller rugs across tables until the end of the century when oriental rugs became more common. Until the middle of the century rush matting was the most common floorcovering because of its draught-insulating properties and because its light colour helped to reflect the sunlight. It, too, came in thin widths to be sewn together

Patchwork and dark panelling *work well together and need warm lighting. The easy arrangement of disparate objects, books and a plant looks casually pretty on the table pictured opposite. The interesting, painted base of the lamp, possibly a converted tea-caddy, looks particularly handsome against the panelling upon which it casts a mellow glow. The leaves of the plant add just the right degree of freshness to the whole vignette.*

A room in grand tradition, *complete with rosy glazed chintz and ruffles, embroidered cushions or pillows, and rugs. The rose sofas of monumental depth look well with the chintz and contrast firmly with the other seating and the brilliant yellow walls, a colour made memorable by Nancy Lancaster and John Fowler in their famous room at 22 Avery Row.*

and was therefore the first form of fitted carpet, but it got dirty quickly and had to be changed every few years. It is interesting that the rushes which had been such a part of medieval floor covering should now be woven into a far more substantial covering, one that, with practical variations and improvements, has lasted in popularity through the centuries. A thinner sort of matting was imported from North Africa or Spain. Pepys was quoted as seeing "a very fine African mat" in London in 1666. At the same time, wood floors were getting more handsome, and people were keeping them bare with an overlay of velvet with a pile like a rug, or with rugs from Persia, Turkey and Cairo. Pile carpet woven in widths as we know it today was not available until the eighteenth century.

English country style *is often thought of as a comfortable mixture of deep, soft seating and chintzes and here is the epitome of that shorthand view with three quite different designs that meld harmoniously together in a corner of a plump sofa.*

The pleasing panelling and pilasters in this old room have been very subtly painted in gentle, subdued tones and form an excellent backdrop for several unforced harmonies. The borders on the curtains combine pleasingly with the patterns on the Chinese vase lamps, and the strong vertical lines of the bureau bookcase with its mirrored doors look well with the curves of the grand piano. Again, the room has just grown over generations with here an addition, there a subtraction, and no very dramatic scheme or colouring.

Discomfort in the seventeenth century

Seventeenth-century chairs were decidedly uncomfortable. Heavy carved-oak chairs have survived from the early periods simply because they were robust, but people mainly had either "back stools" with a rectangular back rest that did not reach down to the seat, which might be covered in anything from plain cloths to velvets and leather; or rush-seated chairs with turned legs. Sometimes two seats were joined together in an early variant of the sofa, and slightly larger versions of "back stools" were made with arms to serve as "great chaires" for the guest or guests of honour or for the host himself. People still showed respect by literally raising an honoured guest above the rest, so "great chaires" had higher seats than the norm and often matching foot stools.

Lilac and off-white panelling *are
an unexpected but charming
combination, subtly outlined with
pure white. The wood is stippled
(see chapter 9) to give added depth
and liveliness of colour, and the
skirting or baseboard is marbled to
simulate the marble of the
fireplace surround, the colours of
which are picked up in the rugs
either side of the hearth.
(Marbling is an English tradition
and is not too difficult to do.
Instructions are given for this
and other painting methods in
chapter 9.)*

Lighting was from candles or primitive oil lamps, though candle-holders in the form of wall sconces, chandeliers and candelabra became increasingly more elaborate. Carved blackamoors holding torchières or candle lights were introduced in Paris in the 1650s and were soon seen in England. They came to be called *guéridons* because of the popularity in France of a black vaudeville actor of that name.

Pictures – mostly portraits, landscapes, maps or engravings – were often hung right on top of tapestries or wall hangings, as were mirrors. When wall hangings gave place to panelling, pictures were hung on top of that, and when gentlemen started to do the grand tour all around Europe, domestic paintings gave way to works of art from the continent. Panelling was usually painted at first, and in quite strong colours, although people also started to use paint to simulate marble and wood-grain.

As always in England, the fireplace formed an important part of the room. Although in the rest of Europe stoves were considered much more practical and efficient, the English seemed to find the sight of blazing logs irresistible, besides which they bolstered the vagaries of the fitful sunlight.

Formality in the eighteenth century
In the eighteenth century chairs started to be properly upholstered and began to be more comfortable. The first sofas and upholstered

Long, graceful windows *looking
out over a gentle garden and
meadows, opposite, are gently
curtained with old lace caught up
in the centre top to form its own
pelmets. Old lace tablecloths or
bedspreads act very well as
curtains or draperies but they
should always be draped, caught
up, or folded, never cut up.
Window seats covered in rose
chintz with room for books and
magazines underneath provide
seating with a view. The squashy
sofa is simply covered to match the
fresh green walls, and the mass of
prints and small paintings
between the windows is balanced
by the variegated prints of the
pillows or cushions resting on the
back of the sofa. Finally, the
matting covered with a large rug
provides comfortable flooring for
this generally very relaxed room.*

A deep, white-painted window *embrasure with its rosy chintz curtains and ruffled pelmet caught with a rosette is balanced at right angles by a large family portrait in a massive gilt frame. The yellow of the stippled walls (see chapter 9) is picked up in the chintz, also covering the deep armchair and cushion with matching ruffles and green piping, and in the yellow border on the rug, although the early chair in the corner strikes a completely unexpected note. The slim glass-based lamp is a good choice right in front of the window. The nineteenth-century Gothic cornice gives crisp delineation. This is a detail of the room shown on page 76.*

Nice old-fashioned chintz *in a yellow, green and white sprigged design covers a screen, neatly braided in yellow and green to match the fabric, and hung with pictures that provide an interesting contrast. The chintz is the same as that used for the curtains elsewhere in the room and also for the sofa pillows. This careful teaming, although the antithesis of the "just happened" school, is a large facet of English country style today, mainly engendered by the late Laura Ashley.*

armchairs were seen, and the rush-bottomed chairs began to acquire squabs. Since many chairs were upholstered in costly fabrics the coverings were detachable, and by the middle of the century loose covers were invented and have remained a staple of British country decoration ever since, as have the flowered chintzes that were introduced. Many of these early (but now battered) chintzes can still be seen in stately homes. Many, too, have been revived and often re-coloured in collections produced by, for example, the National Trust, the late Geoffrey Bennison, Cole's, and Colefax and Fowler (see under Directory of Sources, p. 214).

Wallpaper began to catch on in England around 1730 but came in large sheets rather than rolls. Hand-painted papers with birds, flowers and trees were imported from China, and copied in Europe, and mirror panels became increasingly favoured, as did parquet floors. Divided curtains were in general use and curtains were increasingly elaborate. Pull-up curtains, or Austrian shades, began to be fashionable at this time, as did painted window screens. However, furniture arrangement continued to be stiff and formal.

French doors into the garden *have been commonplace in English country houses since the late eighteenth century when the flow from room to garden became a most fashionable, as well as highly agreeable, trend. Again, this is a detail of the drawing room on pages 76 and 80. The large Chinese urns on stands at either side of the doors make handsome planters and the colours are beautifully picked up in the needlework rug. The long sun-dappled view outside with its great trees and white-painted gate is archetypal England.*

Comfort in the nineteenth century

It was not really until the acceptance of the irregularity and asymmetry of the picturesque style in the early nineteenth century that furniture arrangement came to be more informal and therefore comfortable. This coincided with the arrival of the sofa table for books, sewing, trays of tea and lamps, which made life considerably more convenient, as indeed did the arrival of the round table in the drawing room, usually with its own lamp, around which people sat to chat or play cards by the new, much brighter, oil lamps. Most interiors had dados topped with a chair rail, or moulding, with a different wall treatment above and below. And at about this time the English adopted the double "French doors" that gave easy access to the garden.

A room in the grand manner, sparkling with mirror and long French windows, filled with flowers and plants and colour. The stippled cornices are matched to the curtain fabric, and the stippled walls give a much truer apricot than the best matched flat paint. Note, too, the trompe l'oeil urns above the pelmets, slightly, but endearingly, wobbly.

Original Victorian tiles *in this conservatory are offset by walls covered in a marbled paper devised and prepared by the owners (see chapter 9). It was an extremely successful experiment and makes a splendid background for the various plants, although paper treated by the same method could be used in any other room in a variety of colours.*

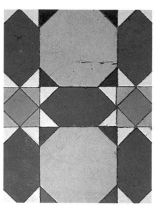

Another Victorian design *has been retained for this distinguished floor with its variation on a diamond theme. Floors like these can be copied in sheet linoleum or tiles of the right subtlety, or in vinyl, with quite spectacular results. An alternative, given patience and a steady hand, is to work out the design on grid paper, then outline it on a base-painted floor and paint it in.*

The rise of the conservatory

After 1845, when the window or glass tax was repealed, conservatories leading off sitting rooms and drawing rooms became very popular. In *Rustic Adornments to Homes of Taste* (1852), Shirley Hibbard pointed out, "where it is advised to keep a few choice birds there can be no better plan than to keep them in separate roomy cages which may be hung up in a conservatory opening from the drawing room. One of these supplied with a small collection of good plants and a dozen cages, each with a pair of breeding canaries, forms a conservatory and aviary combined."

Conservatories became the natural setting for parties and entertainment. The conservatory at Chatsworth, known as the "Great Stove", was lit with 12,000 lamps for an occasion when Queen Victoria drove by in an open carriage. The Duke of Wellington who was there, was moved to pronounce: "I have travelled Europe through and through, and witnessed many scenes of surpassing grandeur on many occasions but never did I see so magnificent a *coup d'oeil* as that extended before me."

In fact conservatories were very splendid adjuncts to a room, filled as they were with exotic plants and ferns which gave off a marvellously evocative scent of damp leaves and the perfume of lilies, jasmine, stephanotis and gardenias. In Benjamin Disraeli's novel, *Henrietta Temple*, a character says that, "It is impossible to live without a conservatory." And Lady Bromley Davenport in her *History of Capesthorne* (1974), reminisces about the conservatory there: "In a magical world of Chinese lanterns, exotic flowers and intoxicating scents, they sipped their wine and laughed and talked, protected by the fragile glass from the cruelty of the winter's night."

The nineteenth-century *conservatory satisfying the newly discovered rage for hothouse plants is a joy in numerous rural houses. The warm, damp smell of these graceful glass constructions has always been a heady one; indeed, many romances in nineteenth-century literature seem to have reached soulful moments in these exotic adjuncts to living rooms. The one opposite, with its glamorous crystal candelabra, can be used for relaxing, reading, what you will. Pale and dark green paint is skilfully mingled with the variegated green of the jungle of plants.*

English style influences the world

In the late nineteenth and early twentieth century the "free" English style was having something of an influence on the rest of Europe and America, and went on doing so, even through the stern tenets of the Bauhaus school which so shaped ideas of decoration and furnishing up to the 1970s. This was a timely reaction against the overcrowding and clutter of Victorian and Edwardian rooms, and its minimal strictures served to pare down the magpie quality inherent in the English decorative style but they never repressed it. Just pre-Bauhaus, the German Hermann Muthesius spread the word in Germany about the unassuming English rural style, and at the beginning of this century several British architects were commissioned to produce in Germany

A butterfly firescreen in front of a strongly figured marble fireplace is only one idiosyncrasy in a room crammed with interesting paintings, prints, objects and memorabilia. The fresh green stippled walls, the unexpected juxtaposition of striped loose covers and chintz, the dense arrangement of art and the whimsical touches all serve to humanize the rather grand and formal room.

A benign English sun *lights up the vinous pattern of these filmy curtains as well as casting intricate shadows on the deep natural pine shutters and the window frame, leaving the rest of the wall space in Rembrandt-like gloom.*

Subtly painted panelling *and a grand fireplace make this room, which is actually quite small, seem much larger than it is. Picking out the chair rail in brown makes the mouldings appear deeper. The glass coffee table reveals the pattern of the needlework rug beneath. The rug and the basket of eggs pick up the colours of the walls, while deep blue sofas make a strong statement.*

the cosy or "quaint" cottage look, exemplified by the same simple rush matting, the sturdy furniture and the comfortable, casual chintz-covered upholstery that is still the trade mark of cottages, farmhouses, rectories and lesser country houses all over Britain.

Looking back, each era in English history has had its own "look", its own feel, and fashions in Europe were picked up remarkably quickly in England – sometimes in a matter of weeks – digested and regurgitated in a uniquely English way. This is not to say that fashion caught on everywhere at the same time. Then, as now, there were arbiters of taste, people who cared enough about fashions to be always at the forefront of changes, and very often these fashions only started to filter down through the various social strata long after the original

A bird and flower chintz, *opposite, frames French doors looking over a terrace to the medieval hall house beyond. The room belongs to a spacious nineteenth-century house built in the grounds of the old house. More birds are framed on the apricot walls, whose warmth is cleverly cooled by the creamy dado and the Holland blind. Note the splendid swan's neck beneath the Regency table.*

progenitors had moved on to new ideas. Moreover, ideas caught on at very different speeds in different localities.

Nevertheless, the same ingredients that we see today, the same sorts of mixtures now overlaid with comfort and airiness, have appeared and reappeared over the centuries. The only really tangible difference is in lighting which has progressed from the horrible harshness of early electricity to the malleable, easily controllable and mellow light of today, with its ability to highlight and accent particular objects, to diminish faults and to exaggerate virtues. If only the average Englishman, the average person, could be weaned from automatically placing a ceiling light in the centre of a living room and calling it lighting, almost every interior would be greatly improved. Uplights placed behind furniture and underneath plants, skilfully placed downlights and spots, practically placed table and reading lamps, will do so very much more to enhance the casual comfort, the gentle prettiness, the quirky eclecticism that are the keynotes and the pride of English country style decoration.

A magnificent grouping *of paintings and some splendid furniture, above right, catch a gentle shaft of sun in a room that always seems sunny thanks to its colouring. Walls are rag rubbed (see chapter 9) with chair rail and baseboard or skirting painted the base colour, cream. The colours of the carpet are repeated in the elaborate curtains and in the fringe at the bottom of the chairs, above left. The sculpture and plants on the table before the French windows lead the eye naturally to the lovely view beyond.*

CHAPTER FOUR

LIBRARIES & STUDIES

Studies serve for delight, for ornament, and for ability.

FRANCIS BACON

A library sitting room, *opposite, in the nineteenth-century tradition: rich, warm colouring, neat built-in bookshelves, comfortable seating and a clubbish-looking fender in front of the fireplace. It is definitely a room to retire to, to relax in, to read and write in. Note the nice detail of the camel stringing in the cornice to match the warm camel of the ceiling, and how the colour is picked up in the sofa fabric.*

An enduring image exists of the English country gentleman deeply ensconced in an armchair beside the fire in his book-lined study. Leather bindings match the battered leather of the upholstery and the room is redolent of years of mellow warmth and comfort. It is an image which almost everyone furnishing a study has in mind and it stems directly from the tradition of the great eighteenth-century country house libraries.

Up until the mid-1600s there were so few books that there was rarely any necessity to have anywhere special to store them. In spite of Francis Bacon's aphorism that "studies serve for delight, for ornament and for ability", and Shakespeare's occasional reference to libraries – "My library was Dukedom large enough," or "Knowing I loved my books he furnish'd me from mine own library with volumes that I prize above my kingdom" – libraries were hardly in existence. Even in a great Elizabethan home like Hardwick, which was so extravagantly

"Books do furnish a room" *as the novelist Anthony Powell, that modern-day Proust, entitled one of his works. Here, a handsomely bound collection of mainly nineteenth- and turn-of-the-century books looks as temptingly eclectic as it is decorative. Who would not envy such a choice country house collection?*

An eighteenth-century painting *depicting Palm Sunday by a Peruvian artist is attached to the handsome bookshelves here to make the focal point. The room is in fact seventeenth-century and although it has undergone vicissitudes over the centuries, the library retains all its early grace and mellowness and is enhanced by the fine leather bindings of the books. The comfortable velvet couch is interestingly backed and trimmed in colours that repeat the shades of the book bindings.*

Engaging personal pictures *are hung casually down the narrow strip of wall next to this handsome and varied collection of books.*

appointed that it is described in detail in almost all scholarly works on English country houses, the 1601 inventory lists only six books, all of them kept in Bess of Hardwick's own bedroom and all of them books for instruction rather than pleasure.

Before the middle of the seventeenth century and again in the nineteenth century, there was something of a social stigma attached to intellectual pursuits in a society where skill first in feats of arms and then in field sports and athletics was more prized than skill in learning, a curious attitude which taints part of the upper echelons of English society even today and is peculiarly British.

The study-closet
By the Restoration period, however, the great increase in curiosity and learning fuelled a similar increase in books, which were usually kept in gentlemen's (not ladies') closets close by the bedroom and dressing room – a custom which is perhaps the origin of the English country house habit of piling books into shelves on landings and in bedroom

corridors. In many cases, small rooms off bedrooms thus became studies with a sturdy table often covered with a green cloth (because then, as now, green was thought to be restful on the eyes), on which was placed a "reading desk", at that time a small piece of furniture with a sloping top.

In the 1660s, when books came out of the closet so to speak, they were first kept on shelves protected by a curtain, and a fringe was often nailed along the edges of the shelves to flick dust off the tops of books when they were taken down.

Libraries for scholarship

Samuel Pepys reputedly had some of the first glass-fronted bookcases. He had twelve of them made between 1666 and his death in 1703. There is a famous drawing belonging to Magdalene College, Cambridge, (famous because pictures of seventeenth-century interiors are rare) showing Pepys's library with five of these bookcases in an otherwise rather empty room, before the time, presumably, when the

Creamy walls and bookshelves,
a needlework rug and coia matting bring a feeling of freshness and light to this room in an old stone farmhouse. Although the furniture and fabrics are traditional, the cheerful filing cabinet and the practical anglepoise lamp beaming down on the open bureau, the row of utilitarian mugs filled with pens and pencils and the capacious cupboards under the shelves turn the room into a good working study, very much of this century but still in keeping with the spirit of the spacious old house.

Eighteenth-century shelves *often had cupboards and secret recesses concealed behind the framework, or jib doors with* trompe l'oeil *books amassed beside the real thing. Here, a twentieth-century set of shelves repeats the same tricks with, this time, a bar concealed behind the mahogany-lined door, complete with floral-patterned round basin set into the bottom shelf and racks thoughtfully provided for wine bottles. The pale terracotta rag-rubbed walls (see chapter 9) contrast well with the book bindings.*

A charming clutter of objects *on this mantelshelf is cheerfully backed by a paper of full-blown roses and an equally diverse series of eclectically chosen pictures.*

other seven were delivered. In the middle of the floor is a table, close-covered or "carpeted" with a cloth, with Pepys's sloping reading desk on top. Above the bookcases are heavily framed portraits.

In the eighteenth century, however, bookcases were very often integrated with the architecture, and it was at this time that the *trompe-l'oeil* habit of concealing ordinary closets and jib doors behind rows of false book spines with dreadful punning titles began. At Chatsworth, the 6th Duke of Devonshire had titles like "Barrow on the Commonweal", "Boyle on Steam" and so on. The propensity to pun, after all, has been as much a part of the English tradition as, say, the English fireplace. In this particular instance, the place of false jocular titles among one of the rarest collections of books in England is a graphic example of the British propensity for irreverence in the midst of scholarship. And there was great scholarship. The eighteenth century was the great era of the English country house library and this well befitted the golden age of enlightenment when the classical education of English gentlemen taught them to appreciate the art of antiquity as much as the necessity for political freedom.

It made a lot of sense for the rich to keep a fine collection of books in their country houses. As Gervase Jackson-Stops points out in his excellent *The English Country House: A Grand Tour* (1985), "There would be leisure to study them, to improve the mind after a day's hunting, perhaps to offer hospitality to a whole circle of *literati* whose erudite conversation would offer parallels with the disputations of the Greek philosophers". Some of the greatest writers and philosophers of the time, Pope, Locke, Gibbon and Burke, were frequent visitors to country house parties, and this familiarity with men of letters in the midst of hunting, shooting, feasting and general rural pursuits encouraged intellectual activity and scientific enquiry even amongst the

A Victorian scrap screen, *in the picture opposite, makes a decorative counterbalance, both in proportion and colours, to the bookcase at right angles to it. Dark green walls are a good background for any study and here are picked up by the shade of the student's lamp on the polished mahogany desk. Screens can be made by pasting illustrated scraps on panels of wood or* papier mâché *to form a dense pattern, usually with a motif of some sort, such as military or naval glory, pastoral life or royalty – as here – and varnishing them thoroughly.*

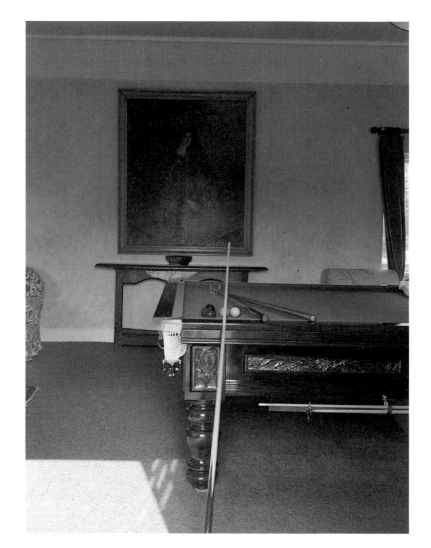

Massive billiards tables *were often placed in libraries in the late eighteenth and early nineteenth centuries but as the years went on they were given their own room, the better for gentlemen to enjoy themselves in an after-dinner game. This table with its carved mahogany base is placed in contrast to the stippled apricot walls (see chapter 9) and the stark lines of the dark oak table underneath the romantic portrait. The carpet is a serviceable mole brown.*

squirarchy. In the summer of 1730, Pope wrote to the 2nd Earl of Oxford, "am impatient to follow you to your new-roofed library and see what fine new lodgings the ancients are to have".

The study and the sitting-library
As the century drew on, however, and merged into the 1800s, this ostensibly male domain began to be invaded by women who turned the room into more of a relaxing family room. Men were thus forced, in the nineteenth century, into smaller versions of the grander libraries, their studies. That indefatigable chronicler and visitor to country houses, Mrs Libbe Powys, writing about Middleton Park, Oxfordshire, remarks that she found: "A most excellent library out of

Leather-bound books *are piled like bricks against the white-painted dado of this vivid hyacinth-coloured room. The strong colour makes an effective background for the modern pictures, and the diamond-patterned matting adds a nice rural feeling as well as forming a contrast to the elaborately carved pediment above the door. Note the deep slope of the ceiling, which denotes a room high under the roof. Note too the graceful depth of the handsome door case.*

the drawing room, seventy foot long – in this room, besides a good collection of books there is every other kind of amusement, as billiards and other tables, and a few good pictures."

Humphry Repton in his *Fragments* (1816) shows a picture of a library with French windows leading into a conservatory. The library is full of people amusing themselves in many different ways and Repton explains that "the most recent modern custom is to use the library as the general living room, and that sort of state room formerly called the best parlour and of late years, the drawing room, is now generally found a melancholy apartment." Repton continued to extol the virtues of "the sitting-library" where family and friends could enjoy different pursuits in a "cultivated but informal" atmosphere.

The wall between the shelves in
this striking little room is an
excellent base for a nicely eclectic
collection of prints, miniatures
and watercolours, not to mention
the old clock around which the
collection pivots. Postcards stuck
nonchalantly here and there
remove any trace of formality, as
does the bustling mantelshelf
above the simple cast iron grate
and small brass fender.

Sir John Soane also describes his own library (and dining room) with evident pleasure. "The general effect of those rooms is admirable. They combine the characteristics of wealth and elegance, taste and comfort with those especial riches which belong expressly to literature and art." His rooms were full of books, statues, classical busts, paintings and rare objects reflected and multiplied by the numerous circular mirrors set around the walls.

The English study: derivations and improvisations
A comprehensive picture of the eclectic late nineteenth-century English study is given by Oscar Wilde in "Pen, Pencil and Poison" when the room belonging to his refined hero, Thomas Griffiths

Bookshelves at right angles *to the window are balanced by a single curtain, in complementary colours to the books, which can be drawn across, as well as by a spectacular little collection of miniatures in equally spectacular gilt frames. This sort of arrangement, like the one shown opposite, can be easily emulated. Note that the radiator is painted to match and blend in with the walls.*

99

Wall-to-wall books, *comfortable seating, warm colouring and a fireplace are all one could want in a library. This one is a good updated version of a library-family room with its television, paintings and generally relaxed air. The fire screen with its arrangement of dried pressed leaves and flowers between sheets of glass looks well with the matting, and the deep colour of the oriental rug balances the rich bindings of the books. Lamps are set at a good height for reading.*

Wainwright, is described: "Wainwright's study was a large room, its floor covered by a Brussels carpet with garlands of flowers. At one end was a desk with a silver inkwell on it and among the other furnishings were a Tomkisson piano, a Grecian couch and a table laden with portfolios of prints. A Damascus sabre hung on one wall and on another was hung a delicious melting love-painting by Fuseli. In one corner of the room there was a fine original cast of the Venus de Medici. Some hot-house plants were lined up on a slab of white marble. On the shelves were books bound in old French Morocco of rare quality. There was an elegantly gilded French lamp with a crystal globe painted with gay flowers and butterflies and the chimney piece was balanced by a large mirror on the opposite wall. Illuminated by that lamp, the room was steeped in a Corregio-like light. In the octagonal boudoir (leading off) there was a Turkish ottoman, and at either side of the fireplace was a chiffonier with a marble top. The crimson walls were partly hidden by a double row of prints gaily framed in rosewood or glossy oak. On the chiffonier was displayed

A true brown study *could be the title of this room, although it is actually one end of a sitting room with library leanings. The large painting of a thoroughly relaxed dog dominates both the bookcases and the comfortable chairs. And the books themselves are comfortably mixed with any number of objects: mugs, tankards, silver cups, china, small paintings, bronzes, boxes, you name it. These are the shelves of inveterate collectors. Note the happy touch of the decorated tin in the shelf below the dog painting. Its pattern is much the same as the armchair beneath it.*

Urbino majolica decorated with reproductions of Raphael's paintings, and other ceramics both biscuit and 'green dragon'."

This description evokes all that typifies the style of an English study, particularly the kind of style that draws upon the opulence of Edwardian country houses. But then any so-called typical English library or study is full of derivations and improvisations from past centuries. The richness of the seventeenth century can be emulated with stripped and dark-stained wood floors and oriental rugs, dark oak bookcases and a certain restrained austerity. The elegant proportions and classic harmony of the eighteenth century can be reproduced in the graceful manner made so popular by John Fowler with either his stripped "dry-scrubbed" look floors and needlepoint rugs, or with rush matting, pedimented and bureau bookcases, light chintzes and comfortable armchairs, skirted occasional tables and the requisite globes and busts. The comfortable, comforting clutter and informality of the nineteenth century lives on with mahogany or stained mahogany shelves, polished or painted panelling, or *faux*-panelling executed

White-painted bricks *and the strong, simple shapes of the andirons in the fireplace set on a black-tiled floor give a decidedly rural look to this little study-sitting room, which is actually in London. The bookshelves are full of objects and mementoes and their painted framework is set off by the grey and white stripe of the mattress ticking loose-cover and the warm colours of the Kelim in front of the mantelpiece. Note the interesting touch provided by the painting of a hat and poetry book on the wall above.*

Stencilling is not usually *associated with English studies, but this example on two-tone pink walls with cream trim gives a light and airy feeling to a small room. (For stencilling instructions, see chapter 9.)*

either with varying shades of paint or with strips of judiciously placed moulding (see chapter 9), club fenders and leather chesterfields and armchairs.

All these, of course, may be mixed with the better offerings and practicalities of our own period, for example: good reading light provided by well-placed and well-designed desk or table lamps, or angled wall lights; and comfortable upholstery (more often than not today's study is fitted with a sleep sofa as a guest bed). Even if there is no actual room for a library or study, there is usually space for a bookish corner *somewhere* in a house or apartment.

Landing spaces make excellent library substitutes. For example, half way up the stairs there is often a small area which can be lined

An old walnut desk *in the same stencilled-walled room provides a good surface for family clutter and stands out effectively against the soft pink ragged walls (see paint techniques, chapter 9), which in turn are nicely set off by the touch of palest green and by the grey carpet.*

Shelves in the twentieth century *are more often than not used for memorabilia as well as books – family photographs, old postcards, bits of porcelain, objects of vertu, small clocks and boxes, perhaps a plant or two. This gives them an informality that was often lacking in former centuries, and adds lightness and a familial feel to bookcases that could otherwise seem quite grand, such as those shown here. They line a wall of a beautifully proportioned eighteenth-century room and although most of the books are handsomely bound in leather, the pictures and objects interspersed among them capture the spirit of those nineteenth-century libraries which became as much family rooms as libraries proper. The two-tone paintwork of apricot and cream, with the darker paint applied between the mouldings, adds further grace to the beauty of the shelves.*

An eccentric painting *of beflowered, top-hatted and frock-coated gentlemen with monkeys on a brilliant green sward, neatly framed in bird's eye maple, is the kind of charmingly bizarre subject to be stumbled upon in many country houses.*

Mahogany and black marble
*are handsome ingredients in the
hall-library opposite. The
mahogany shelves are in fact
mahogany-stained rather than
the real thing and look none the
worse for that, for they are still
handsome. The blue and white
Dutch tiles were discovered behind
a sheet of boarding, whilst the
marble was uncovered beneath
coats of cream paint. The flower-
pot painted walls and the coia
matting make a warm
background for the gilded
nineteenth-century chairs caught
in the indirect light from the
uplights judiciously placed in
corners.*

with shelves and which may even be large enough to accommodate a desk as well. Larger landing spaces may take a library table or equivalent between the shelves.

Occasionally there is room right under the staircase for shelves and a desk. And certainly, an entire hallway can be lined with shelves from painted wood to grander mahogany or oak. The space around and below bedroom windows also has good book potential. Shelves can be fitted to the wall space and a desk top can be built all along the window wall with filing cabinets underneath, or an old writing table-cum-dressing table can be used. There is, too, nothing wrong with a book-lined dining room, which perforce makes for a mellow atmosphere. If the books have handsome tooled bindings, they will look particularly well in the glow of a candle-lit dinner. And bookshelves and desks in sitting rooms are, of course, commonplace.

In whatever guise, the sitting-library, the bookish sitting room, the book-lined landing or dining room, lives on as part of the great English country house tradition.

Stair landings are good places
*for continuing a library, especially
in country houses where space is
generally more generous. Here,
creamy bookshelves have been
fitted above radiators covered in
fretwork panels. The plain
cornflower walls are an excellent
foil for the elaborate pediments
over the doors and are matched by
the flowing tablecloth with its
striped top, which in turn matches
the shade at the window. One
good idea – not, however,
normally associated with libraries
– is separate baskets for each
child's laundry.*

107

CHAPTER FIVE

DINING ROOMS

I like fine old rooms that have been occupied in a fine old way.

HENRY JAMES *writing in 1873*

A spectacular stone floor *laid with white marble, as pictured opposite, could be emulated, though not so grandly, in linoleum or vinyl or faux wood tiles (see chapter 9). This dining hall is a magnificent mixture of centuries with its early oak-panelled screen and rusticated arches harking back to the screens passage of medieval times. In fact this early house was Georgianized in the late eighteenth century and the whole space converted into a single lofty room. It was divided again by the screen in this century to create better proportion.*

ith its massive mahogany table and sideboard, rich dark walls and gleaming silver, the dining room seems so much a part of the English country house that it is odd to think that a room just for eating was really an eighteenth-century invention. One of the first rooms formally called a dining room was designed by William Kent in 1732 for Sir Robert Walpole's house, Houghton Hall, in Norfolk.

Before the dining room

In the Middle Ages people sat at trestle tables in the Great Hall, and later the gentry sat in the soler. Tudors and Elizabethans who lived in substantial country houses ate in the great chamber or the saloon, or in small rooms off, and seventeenth-century people of any standing normally dined in the parlour, while the rest of the population ate in the kitchen. After the Middle Ages, walls in these general living rooms were commonly panelled with wood that was either painted or

Stripped Victorian pine *is used here to great effect against cloudy rag-rubbed walls (see chapter 9) and the elaborate frame of this cupboard is nicely balanced by the simple lines of the glasses. The dining room in which it is hung is shown on pages 120-21.*

109

grained or marbled in dark colours. Or they were hung with tapestries or fabrics battened to the wall with the nails covered with fillets of gilded leather or painted wood.

Floors were covered in rush matting and occasionally with oriental carpets, but there was seldom a permanent dining table, most tables being brought forward from the side of the room and set up in the centre when necessary. They did, however, have side tables consisting of tiered "cup-boards", or buffets, on which cups, drinking vessels and plate were displayed and from which wine and food were served. Nearby, there would also be a wine cooler made from copper or marble, or even sometimes of silver, in which wine and water could be kept at a steady temperature.

Pale terracotta ragged walls *(see chapter 9) allied to coia matting and a pale Samarkand rug soften the formality of the oval Sheraton mahogany table and the Regency chairs in this old farmhouse dining room. Here, the room is lit almost entirely by candles.*

An old patchwork quilt *used as a tablecloth, in the same room as that pictured opposite, is set next to a much less formal nineteenth-century bamboo chair with a chintz squab. The carved Chippendale eagle surmounting the painting adds a dramatic note to the otherwise sedate and gentle space.*

By the end of the seventeenth century, the smaller the company at a meal, the greater was the honour, in direct contrast to previous decades when large rooms were needed to house great hosts of people. Meals were now set up on occasional tables wherever people had a mind to take them: in the bedroom, the saloon, or the parlour, and caned chairs were brought to the table from their places against the walls. These occasional tables were generally oval or round with gate legs and folding leaves. By the 1700s, the tiered cupboards had gone out of fashion and were replaced by the now ubiquitous side table or sideboard, at that time often topped with marble or stone. They were generally very handsome and often surmounted by a splendid mirror flanked by candle sconces.

A distinguished early portrait in a handsome oval frame looks very striking against the mellow panelling of this old room; and hung as it is over the intricately carved and inlaid side table with its collection of china, the painting contributes to a pleasing still-life. Better still, the room seems like a time freeze of the seventeenth century with its discreet richness of objects and colouring and its heavy but well-modelled shapes and curves.

The male dining room

England was really the first European country to eschew this flexibility and design rooms especially for eating. Robert Adam, in his introduction to his plans for the remodelling of Syon House, explained that the English had to pay attention to such rooms because, "accustomed by habit, or induced by the nature of our climate, we indulge more largely in the enjoyment of the bottle". "The eating rooms", he went on, betraying that male chauvinism that afflicted the British for centuries, "are considered as the apartments of conversation in which we [meaning men] are to pass a great part of our time – this renders it desirable to have them fitted up with elegance and splendour, but in a style different from that of other apartments. Instead of being hung with damask, tapestry etc", he explained practically, "they are always finished with stucco, and adorned with statues and paintings, that they may not retain the smell of victuals."

In the same vein he added that, "Soon after dinner the ladies retire ... Left alone, they [the men] resume their seats, evidently more at

"Few colours look better than a deep crimson" *said that arbiter of taste, J. C. Loudon, in his* The Surburban Gardener and Villa Companion *published in 1838, and this room with its nice solid mahogany, its marquetry longcase clock and exquisite mirror reflecting the deep greens outside is an excellent example. In fact, so green and dense is the foliage around the deep-set window that the candles look right as an extra booster, even in broad daylight.*

ease, and the conversation takes a different turn – less reserved – and either gayer or more licentious". It seems that not only the conversation was less reserved. Louis Simond, a Frenchman normally living in New York, and author of *Journal of a Tour and Residence in Great Britain during the years 1810 and 1811,* was evidently shocked by the habit in certain circles of keeping in a corner of the dining room a chamber pot which was apparently quite unconcernedly used as needed, with no breaks in the conversation. "Will it be credited", he wrote, "that, in a corner of the very dining room there is a certain convenient piece of furniture to be used by anybody who wants it." Slightly more discreetly, Sheraton himself, when explaining his furniture, described how the left-hand drawer of a sideboard was sometimes made very short to make room for a pot cupboard below.

Dining rooms in the eighteenth century often included a pair of pedestals topped with urns that sometimes served as cisterns for water in which glasses could be rinsed. Alternatively, a pedestal itself might contain a lead-lined drawer that could be used as a rinsing basin, or it

A generously wide windowsill *with a collection of blue and white pottery, including soup tureens filled with pot pourri and plants, a jug and a ginger jar, forms a pleasant little still-life in this farmhouse room, especially when backed by the old stone walls and tiled roofs of the farm buildings beyond. Warm pinky-beige curtains are edged with a matching twisted braid and double lined to add warmth to the room at night.*

might hold a metal-lined drawer with a small heater for warming plates. The traditional long table did not become a permanent fixture until about the 1780s. Yet only 70 years or so later we find Archdeacon Grantly in Anthony Trollope's *Barchester Towers* (1857) saying, "there is something democratic and parvenu in a round table".

Dinner in daylight

In the early part of the eighteenth century, colour schemes tended to be quite dark and rich, for the neo-Classical architects who had studied the buildings of ancient Rome in such detail could not help but be influenced by the vivid colours of latter-day Rome as well. Lighter schemes in the French mode began to appear after 1750, and again this was practical, for since dinner was generally served around 2 p.m. the room was mainly used in daylight. As the century wore on, the dinner hour started to creep on too so that, by the Regency era when dinner was taken in the early evening, luncheon had to be introduced to fill the gap.

The damask is nicely rumpled *after a winter lunch in the elegant eighteenth-century room pictured opposite. Although grandly proportioned and overtly formal with its large tapestry, deep cornice, handsome chandelier and elaborately draped and trimmed curtains, this dining room is nevertheless made comfortable and even light-hearted by the deeply upholstered armchairs and plentiful flowers—massed tulips and luxuriant azaleas, and rose trees in blue and white pots.*

Deep red damask walls *and a splendid candelabra over the ebony inlaid Regency table give the dining room pictured opposite a seductive feel, which is heightened by the contrast between the deep red hues of the walls and curtains and the fresh greens of the rolling view from the window. The black-framed chairs are interestingly covered with an embroidered canvas in a grape design and, in contrast, the comfortable looking window seat is covered in a cream, brown and blue stripe.*

At this time, also, elaborate plasterwork and panelling in some of the grander houses started to be replaced by mouldings worked in *papier mâché*, a short-cut that was also very much cheaper. The paintings that were hung were mainly portraits, still-lives of food, fruit and dead game, and, in the nineteenth century, the sporting and animal paintings that became such a trademark of the British.

Most rooms had dados topped with chair rails, but by the nineteenth century the space above began to be covered in cloth or in paper again and sometimes the dado was dropped altogether. George Smith in his *Collection of Designs for Household Furniture and Interior Decoration* (1808) says that "superfine cloth or cassimere will ever be the best for 'eating rooms' and libraries where a material of more substance is requisite than for rooms of lighter cast". He adds that crimson or scarlet are best, and that if calico is to be used it must be of one colour in shades of maroon or scarlet.

Dark, "massive and simple"

The fashion for reds and darker colours used so often for modern dining rooms and studies began soon after 1800. J. C. Loudon in his *The Suburban Gardener and Villa Companion* (1838) mentions that "few colours look better than a deep crimson paper in flock, the ceiling and cornice tinted to match". These flock papers were so popular that they became known as "English" papers in Europe and were especially fashionable in France. Loudon also advocated a wood fire with large logs; a chimney surround of dove-coloured, black, and black and yellow, marble; chairs covered in crimson leather with silk tufts; and an easy chair placed on each side of the fire. In a closet, he added, "should be the utensils sometimes required by a gentleman after dinner. This closet should have thick walls and should be large enough

Another red dining room, *in traditional seventeenth-century mode, with dark oak furniture, tapestry chair seats, a nicely battered carpet, oak dresser or hutch and mandatory sporting print. The table is even set for tea, that most English of country meals. Extra chairs, this time more rustic, with elm frames and rush seats, are lined up against the window wall.*

Felicitous juxtapositions *like this are the highlights of decoration. The green and purple of the glass decanters blend happily with the painted design of the plate above, and look good reflected in the polished surface of the marquetry side table with its intricate border.*

This farmhouse dining room, *also pictured opposite, was probably at one time two separate spaces, judging by the two fireplaces, one of which (see opposite) is much smaller than the other and is now a useful storage cupboard; the other, considerably taller, probably served as both oven or range and fire. The simple room is marvellously rewarding with its lovely collection of old jelly moulds and stone mortars, its simple white plates and cheese stand and fluted white ceramic candlesticks. The shining black jugs give an almost psychodelic feel to the prevailing whiteness.*

for a person to stand in." At least this was an improvement on the barely disguised utensil so deplored by poor Monsieur Simond some 30 years earlier. It was also the start of the English cloakroom, or American powder room, which gave such rein to the imagination from the nineteenth century onwards.

It is significant that writers on interior precepts were constantly mentioning the gentlemen's convenience with little mention of women, for they seemed to agree that the dining room needed a masculine air. Robert Kerr in *The Gentleman's House* (1864) states that, "The whole appearance of the [dining] room ought to be that of masculine importance so the decor should be somewhat massive and simple." He goes on to suggest that there should always be a sideboard on which the owner's plate could be displayed, and in the recesses flanking the fireplace should be two "dinner waggons". He also mentions that it is sometimes "the practice to place the chairs, or a portion of them when not in use, not against the wall, but around the table", which is of course our modern custom.

Battered old white walls, *opposite and in another view above left, are far removed from the polished mahogany, silver and candelabra of the average English country house dining room. Nevertheless, this sympathetic room is all the better for being unashamedly bucolic. The simple whitewash, the old grey flagstones on the floor and the solid white of the woodwork – apart from the splendidly fluorescent green around the far door – make the eggplant or aubergine colour of the chairs and the collection of purple glass and china on the shelves of the dresser look twice as rich.*

A detail of the Victorian dresser, *pictured right, with its flamboyantly carved uprights and more chastely carved shelves. It makes a capacious storage unit as well as showing off to advantage the collection of china and the odd pieces of silver such as sauce boats and wine coasters.*

Complicated Victorian *furniture looks unexpectedly splendid in this dining room setting with its cloudy rag-rolled walls, glazed to reduce the blue to the right subtlety, and its stripped and polished floor (see chapter 9). The pine chair rail all round the room helps to lower the ceiling height and the extra-deep skirting or baseboards give the room a feeling of great solidity, as, of course, do the furniture and the hefty marble fireplace. Blue and white plates on the dresser or hutch shelves, with cups adding touches of yellow, the pink hyacinths, and the soft toning colouring of the flamestitch upholstery and the rugs stand out well against the predominant grey-blues and pale wood of the room.*

The fireplace end *of the spacious dining area shown on the previous pages. Note the interesting swirling details of the rag-rubbed walls (see chapter 9) and the nice balance of the large pine mirror above the marble fireplace with its inset blue and white tiles. The heavy marble is also a foil for the glass and silver candlesticks on the wide mantelshelf.*

Window curtains had been eschewed in the eighteenth century, along with wall fabrics, but became enormously popular again in the nineteenth century, and with all sorts of variations: "Window curtains," says Loudon again, "give the mistress of the house an excellent opportunity for exercising her taste in their arrangement." But most interesting, in view of the current belief that the lynch pin of English decoration is English chintz, is the general dismissal of that fabric. Cassell's *Household Guide*, published in the early 1860s, states that, "All kinds of damask, moreen and rep will, for wear and effect, be preferable to chintz." It was not, in fact, until the late 1920s and 30s that the interest in chintzes was revived. Up to the 1870s, too, people building houses tended to want their interiors to look new, fresh and unworn. But antiques came into demand with the beginning of the "Queen Anne" fashion, with its penchant for irregularity and asymmetrical arrangement. Colour schemes were so much more mellow that they needed faded wood, and for the first time wear and tear came to be admired rather than derided.

Ribboned braces of game, *entwined fish, leonine gargoyles and bunches of grapes, pears and pineapples are among the lavish carvings of this high Victorian piece. A decade or so ago it might well have been scorned but not in the England of the eighties. Here, with its grandiose pediment backed with lavish sprays of dried flowers and grasses, it is a very splendid part of the dining room.*

Graceful glazed doors *open on to a pebbled yard from this subtly detailed eating end of a farmhouse kitchen. Stone frames round the doors and window harmonize with the old stone walls outside, and the unusual wood skirting or base-boards match the threshold, shelves, chair rail and windowsill. White-painted window frames and doors freshen the dairy cream of the walls and the whole is nicely balanced by the practical cork floor. A pleasant collection of jugs and platters is stashed neatly but decoratively above the door and window. The whole feeling of the room is one of serene restraint.*

Dining by electricity

The latter part of the nineteenth century saw the biggest revolution of all in interior design: the invention first of the gas light, which had become widespread by the 1870s, and then, in 1879, of the electric light bulb. For a while, the idea of lighting the table with electricity was the most delightful of novelties. In the late 1920s, in *The Whole Art of Dining* J. Rey announced: "The old-fashioned wax candles of glittering propensity which so often alarmed the guests and were most annoying during dinner, by the ornamental shades taking fire, have long disappeared from all well-appointed tables". But electric light was too harsh. Until the advent of the dimmer switch, the *cognoscenti* went back to candles for table lighting. As Thomas Walker, a Regency gourmet, had observed, "There is no art in lighting a table by cum-brous branches, but there is in throwing a light upon it, like some Rembrandt paintings, and the effect is accordingly. The first is vulgar; the latter refined. The art of throwing the most agreeable light upon a table is well worth cultivating."

Brightly painted plaster *was very much a country tradition once paint took over from wall hangings and in fact vivid colouring like that in the dining room pictured opposite is often more in keeping with old houses than the more conventional black and white. Whatever the arguments, the saffron is undeniably handsome with the strong, dark lines of the exposed beams, and shows off the colour and shape of the furniture, the glass and the china in a quite dramatic way. The juxtapositon of the simple rustic refectory table with the other furniture is also interesting, as is the practical carpet-tiled floor with its deep green colouring, and the gros point embroidered seat on the long stool.*

A fresh green tablecloth *looks dazzling against the dark timber and strong curved arch of the doorway here. Simple latticed wallpaper makes a good background for the plants and, indeed, for the strongly embroidered chair seats, as well as making a quiet frame for the rural view outside.*

The contemporary country dining room

Although radical changes in furnishing and decorating were being advocated in Europe and America, particularly in Austria and Germany by architects like Josef Hoffmann, Otto Wagner and Leopold Bauer with their severe and uncompromisingly geometric Secession School (based, to some extent, on the work of Charles Rennie Mackintosh and the Glasgow School), most people in Britain at the turn of the century favoured the comfortable neo-Georgian look. This look, combining late eighteenth-century antiques, or re-productions, with the pared-down late Victorian arrangement and the Edwardian sense of comfort, appealed to both the established and those who could afford to aspire to the establishment. It was a look which not only found favour in less progressive parts of Europe, but in America and the Dominions as well, and it is the basis of the English country style of today. For it was revived after World War II together with a re-born enthusiasm for country houses, the late eighteenth century and the more romantic aspects of the Regency.

Old, weathered boarding *and a terracotta tiled floor form a solid background for the 1930s cane chair with its soft chintz cushions in disparate floral patterns. The pinky-lilac tones of the chair look particularly good against the battered boards and the darker tone of the floor.*

Unexpected blue walls *– such colour is rare in English dining rooms – show off the handsome cornice, door cases and fireplace in this large and elegant room. The colour also looks marvellous with the green outside, reflected in the mirror, and with the interesting black and white horse pictures. The chair rail and the soft, neutral carpet nicely break up the blue, which looks good in both summer and winter: cool in one season and sparkling with firelight in the other.*

The ingredients for a contemporary English country dining room complete with its look of "pleasing decay", a phrase the late John Fowler was fond of using, but which, as we have seen, dated only from the late nineteenth century, might combine some, or perhaps all, of these ingredients from the past: the mahogany table and sideboard, the urns and wine coolers, comfortable wide-seated chairs or cane-seated chairs, polished floors and rugs battered by years of children and dogs, and curtains of varying degrees of elaboration and dilapidation. Walls might be dadoed, or panelled (or false panelled), or covered in deep-coloured hessian or some other cloth, or dragged, or grained, or marbled with mouldings picked out in subtle shades and tints. Reds in one shade or another continue to be used, as do dark greens or blues, colours that were favoured by the eighteenth century and in any case provide good background tones for food and antique furniture.

But now too, there might well be an element of Victoriana and Edwardiana, particularly the "downstairs" and rural offerings of the

The handsome Empire piece *here has been totally tamed and domesticated by the collection of teapots placed on top of it. Note the configuration of beams and plaster with the comparative sophistication of the herringbone parquet floor and the brass ornamentation of the cabinet.*

nineteenth century: the sturdy pine tables and armoires, the rush-seated country chairs, the rush matting and old brick or pammented floors of the Victorian farmhouse, combined with the converted oil and gas lamps of the turn of the century. Rural style, after all, is not entirely confined to the eighteenth- and nineteenth-century English country house, for people are now beginning to admire the sturdiness and looks of furnishings emanating from the farm and cottage as well as from the domestic quarters of the grander houses.

Then again, these more lowly Victorian and Edwardian elements might well be mixed with an earlier piece from the seventeenth century: an old chest, a turned chair, a corner cupboard, old iron candlesticks or wall sconces, preferably with proper candles but in many cases false electrified "candles" with shades.

One thing is certain, however, that whatever the contemporary ingredients turn out to be, the style is in the mix, and always it has to be seen against the frame of English light and English fields, English trees and English gardens.

CHAPTER SIX

KITCHENS

*The windows were wide open and there was a delicious scent
of wallflowers and tea and cake and cobbler's wax.*

FLORA THOMPSON, *Lark Rise to Candleford*

An old iron grate and surround,
*opposite, has a copper kettle at the
ready and neat tiles at the side
encroaching on to the black hearth
tiles below. Baskets full of twigs,
old leaves and boughs of rosemary
for aromatic kindling look
cheerfully rural, and the jade
green walls, old mirror, simple
mantelshelf arrangement and
wide polished floorboards all
combine to make this a very
pleasant room indeed.*

ou expect in a rural English house to come across
cool stone larders with rows of home-made jams
and preserves and muslin bags of jelly dripping
into earthenware bowls; to see mounds of produce, still earthy from the kitchen garden, forming unselfconscious still-lives on sturdy, scrubbed
wood tables. You think of neat stacks of plates in
the china cupboard; arrays of blue and white china on the dresser or
hutch; baskets stacked on flagged stone or brick floors, or swinging
from the beams. There will be the glow of a fire, the gleam of brass and
copper, and the delectable smell of baking bread.

Even the term country kitchen is so evocative of all those old-
fashioned, anomalous rural virtues of thrift and largesse, hard work
and relaxation, temperance and jollity that it is difficult to reconcile
these associations with the fact that until the 1920s most well-to-do
families possessed kitchens that they hardly ever thought of, let alone
visited. The kitchen was for the servants and above all for the cook.

A small round copper basin,
*sunk into a grooved butcher's
block has a neat upstand of
moulded pine which is unusually
put together, rather like bricks.
The wooden doors below are again
interestingly detailed with darker
frames. The pale tawny colour of
the wood looks particularly good
against the stormy blue of the
walls.*

129

Children's size furniture *is frequently very decorative and can look good interspersed amongst the norm. Here, an old green-painted piece forms a nice contrast with the pale yellow of the wall behind and the squared design of the sophisticated wood block floor.*

Liberty willow print cotton *looks effective with the toning coloured border around the windows and under the cornice in this cheerful eating area. The painted jugs on the door panels are echoed by a collection of the real thing-balanced on the door case above, just as the cane chairs are repeated in the painting by the doorway. The wall lamps above the amiable clutter on the ledge behind the settle add an unexpectedly exotic touch in such a room.*

The farmhouse influence

Our nostalgia, then, is less for country house kitchens than for the larders and kitchens of farmhouses and cottages where for centuries they were in fact general living rooms. Where I grew up the water for the kitchen had to be pumped up from a well twice a day by a neat wooden pump with iron fittings, set conveniently next to the sloping earthenware sink with its scrubbed wood draining board. You had to pump back and forth for half an hour or so at a time. There was a cast iron kitchen range set in the old fireplace opening, with an oven on one side of a central fire and the boiler for the hot water on the other. The washing was done in an old copper set into a white-painted brick frame, and next to that was a cast iron and wood mangle for drying the clothes, with a door and a step down to the larder beyond. The floor was of rosy red brick with a rag rug in front of the blacked range, and there was a large scrubbed wood table under a windowsill set with geraniums. There were elm chairs with rush seats, a rocking chair in front of the fire, and Suffolk cured hams, bunches of thyme and sage

and rosemary swinging from the beams. There always seemed to be something simmering on top of the range (which was later supplemented by a Calor gas stove), great saucepans of jam, or soup, or stew, and the fire had constantly to be fed with coal or anthracite, the cinders razzled out with a long iron rod with a sort of hook on the end.

All these details are etched on my mind for I loved the atmosphere of that room, and the fearsome, but not too fearsome, ritual at night of lighting the oil lamps and carrying them from shadowy room to shadowy room, for we had no electricity in the village till the 1950s. Moreover, as I now know, the equipment, apart from the luxury of taps, was substantially that of the classic English rural kitchen for generations, and certainly the model for the nostalgic kitchen of today, give or take the infiltration of sophisticated appliances to ease the loss of servants: stoves with convector ovens that heat at the touch of a switch, microwaves, deep freezers and mammoth refrigerators, ice cream makers, toasters, food processors, dishwashing and washing machines and dryers.

Suffolk pink-plastered walls, *a pale brick floor and a nice old brass-bound stove (with a separate modern hob on the new brick plinth) are handsomely offset by the green Mexican tiles and the pine doors. The mirror on the right-angled wall reflects another window and thus adds more light to the space.*

131

Victorian glass rolling pins *were very often used as love tokens for sailors, hence the frequent maritime verses and expressions or symbols. The blue Bristol glass variety are particularly prized and one here forms the bottom of the small group attached to the battered brick wall of this country kitchen. Such walls inevitably make good backgrounds for all sorts of objects and artefacts like old kitchen utensils, ginger bread moulds, etc.*

The "sterile laboratory"

Nor is it so odd that the kitchen has endured in its essentials for so long. Mario Praz, that distinguished arbiter of decorating, wrote in his classic *An Illustrated History of Interior Decoration* (1964): "The kitchens and little dining rooms of humble people have always been, even down to our own day, the most conservative among rooms. In them, the functional always prevails over the ornamental, and frequently one may even say that decoration does not exist at all. Who has not seen in country kitchens before the last war those gleaming displays of copper utensils? The spacious hearth with andirons and spit, the table with a still life of crockery and food, the china cupboard with plates in neat array – these are the things which until yesterday were timeless, but electrical appliances have transformed the dark, aromatic kitchen into a luminous and sterile laboratory."

In fact, Mr Praz was not the first to talk about the kitchen becoming a laboratory: one hundred years earlier, Robert Kerr in *The Gentleman's House* (1864) mentioned that the kitchen in a large country house has "the character of a complicated laboratory", with all its sophisticated ranges, although his tone was admiring rather than gloomy. And Mr Praz was unduly gloomy, although his strictures certainly applied to the greater proportion of British middle and upper class homes in the 1950s, 60s and early 70s with their rush to modernize at all costs. For, having reached the stage where the kitchen seemed more to resemble an operating theatre than a comfortable, comforting place in which to cook, with food carefully concealed behind prim doors (as opposed to Mario Praz's description of a room where "all the contents are in the open, clearly visible and a series of rustic natural still lives cover the shelves") and cooking smells minimized by air extractors, we arrived at the bizarre stage of importing

Stripped-down brick walls *make a warm background for this kitchen-dining room, opposite, with its long refectory table, old Irish bookcase used to store and display china and glass, old dresser or hutch bases used instead of modern units, and nice wood ceiling laid on the same diagonal as the brick floor (outside the picture). Generous baskets of plants hang from the skylight above the table, and blue and white French tiles – used both for the shelf and the splash-back – tie in nicely with the blue and white platters, which are as much a favourite in English kitchens as they are elsewhere. The ancient wooden mortar in the foreground, used now for salt, could be early English but in fact is pre-Columbian, and the old kitchen chairs are the kind that can be picked up for a song at junk shops and either stripped or painted.*

Nicely battered pine shutters *are gently offset by lace curtains and stripped and polished floor boards in this pleasant kitchen, left. Together they make an effective background for assorted baskets of fruit and vegetables set on the floor and the marble top.*

Dressers or hutches *as they are called in America are a much prized part of an English country kitchen whether of stripped pine, as here, or painted and glazed with panes of glass. This one, mainly because it is backed by a gently rosy wall, seems positively to glow with its collection of rose-rimmed plates and pink mugs along with all the blue and white. Even the coxcomb of the pottery chicken ties in with the general scheme, as do the flowers planted in a blue and white terrine. The pine table and nice old country chairs in the foreground make a comfortable place to eat and the particularly ornate black and gold dome looks well against their plainness.*

Chaste blue and white tiles look quite spectacular against the stone-framed window in this seventeenth-century house. The sun dapples palely through the mullions on to the pine windowsill and down to the slate counter below. The old blue and white jugs on the somewhat battered shelf look pleasing against the golden pine and the walls, which subtly match the bleached tawny colour of the massive window frame.

Wall-mounted wooden plate *racks are very much a farmhouse tradition and are generally as practical as they are sturdily good-looking, for plates can be stored as well as left to dry. Here, they form a nice contrast to the plaster walls and the old salt container mounted just below the rack and in just the right place for easy access to cooking utensils.*

such decorative touches as strings of plastic onions and garlic and plastic surfaces emulating wood – all with the false idea of bringing a rustic look back to the kitchen.

And back to the country

Happily, the old status quo has re-established itself, mostly due to increased travel, the cook book revolution and the consequent interest in cooking and appreciation of honest, time-tested accessories and kitchen equipment. The rural kitchen of today *will* almost certainly contain the scrubbed wood table and the dresser or hutch stacked with china and collectibles that were *de rigueur* for so long. There will be plants and herbs on the windowsills, sturdy country chairs, small patterned country fabrics or checks, plaster or stripped or painted-brick walls, hard floors, probably an Aga stove supplemented by electricity and gas to replace the old range, an electric spit, bunches of herbs and onions and garlic, serried ranks of storage jars, and perhaps an oil lamp or two supplemented by background and direct lighting.

A vast collection *of jugs, mugs, plates, cups and other pieces of assorted china balanced on dresser shelves and mantelpiece is the dominant feature of this splendid room. But the long refectory table looks handsome with the lighter chestnut chairs, as does the dark quarry-tiled floor and the cavernous fireplace. The juxtapositon of rose walls with the dark cream, shiny woodwork is also interesting. Note the Edwardian glass-shaded lamp suspended from one corner of the dresser or hutch which successfully and dramatically illuminates so much of the very eclectic collection.*

From the middle ages to the 1860s

Although it is difficult to trace farmhouse and cottage interiors back much further than the 1700s, documentary evidence of kitchens in great houses shows that they changed very little from medieval times to the 1860s. Cooking was done on open fires, at first on an open hearth and then in cavernous fireplaces, and particularly well-appointed houses had at least three such fireplaces: one for spits, one for boiling, and the third containing a primitive brick oven for baking. The smoke, heat, and smell of the spit-roasting was close to over-powering, especially in the larger houses, and, in an attempt at ventilation, kitchens were built with very lofty ceilings. Mark Girouard in his invaluable *Life in the English Country House* (1978) quotes orders

An old pine dresser base *topped with a chunk of marble makes a subtle room divider between the kitchen area shown here and the dining end shown on pages 120-21, as well as acting as a sideboard and general dumping surface. Almost all of the furniture and accessories in the room, down to the wooden plate racks hanging on the wall, are nineteenth-century but the kitchen works none the less well for that.*

Another facet *of the splendid kitchen-dining area shown opposite and on pages 120-21. The original tiled floor, seen through the door, has been left untouched, as have all the other natural ingredients in this house, and the cleverly rag-rubbed walls only add to the golden richness of the plethora of pine.*

in Henry VIII's household that kitchen scullions who did the really dirty, smoky work by the spits and cleaned the dishes afterwards, "should not go naked or in garments of such vileness as they now do". Sometimes, though, spits were turned by specially trained short-legged dogs locked in cages set in the wall. The dogs were forced to pad interminably round and round to retain their balance.

Floors were first plain, well-trodden earth and then stone-flagged. In large houses there was always a great trestle table or two, and later on there were dressers or hutches and perforated wooden cupboards called "aumbries" for food, eating utensils and linen (this last kept well away from the smoke in a separate linen room). Pots and pans and cooking utensils were hung from racks, and sides of bacon, hams,

dried fish, salt beef and strings of onions and bunches of herbs from the rafters. In the 1680s many builders moved the kitchen away from the main block into a separate outhouse or pavilion, with the notion that the removal of the smells would be well worth the inconvenience (and cold food). At this time, too, a rudimentary kitchen range was introduced which again changed very little until Victorian times when the closed range was pioneered. But the Victorians, like earlier generations, thought it more important to keep cooking smells away from the main rooms than to have warm food. They therefore placed the kitchen as far away from their living quarters as possible, installing louvers in kitchen roofs and various turns and kinks in long service corridors to try to ensure the absence of any cooking odour.

A dazzling array of flowers *and grapes has been painted on nearly all the door panels in this covetable, buttery walled kitchen, with its doughty scrubbed table, green floor and shelves full of mugs and baskets.*

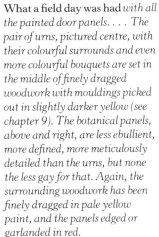

What a field day was had *with all the painted door panels. . . . The pair of urns, pictured centre, with their colourful surrounds and even more colourful bouquets are set in the middle of finely dragged woodwork with mouldings picked out in slightly darker yellow (see chapter 9). The botanical panels, above and right, are less ebullient, more defined, more meticulously detailed than the urns, but none the less gay for that. Again, the surrounding woodwork has been finely dragged in pale yellow paint, and the panels edged or garlanded in red.*

Gas and electric cookers

The first gas stove was shown at the Great Exhibition in London in 1851 but did not really come into its own until a decade or so later. Indeed, the flat-topped, cast iron kitchen range of the 1860s trailed on in remoter country areas until well into the early post-World War II years. Kettles and pots came off their hooks, heavy iron cooking pots began to be replaced by lighter ware of coated steel, and, with the beginning of piped water, there was at least a little store of hot water with which to wash dishes. The first real revolution in the kitchen, though, came with the exhibition of the first clumsy, almost unrecognizable electric cooker in the Chicago Columbia exhibition of 1893. This filtered through to Britain and Europe with comparative speed,

141

A large mounted salmon trophy *surmounts the Aga, that bastion of English country cooking, in another part of the room pictured opposite. Agas, at first fired by anthracite and now by oil or gas, provide four ovens at differing temperatures and are eminently practicable for country house entertaining. Cream-painted cupboards are matched by cream tiles with the odd pale green flower, which team with the wallpaper. The sturdy brick floor adds warmth to the creams, greens and white as well as being hard wearing enough to withstand the worst onslaughts of muddy boots, children and dogs.*

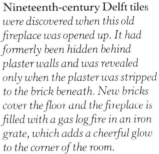

Nineteenth-century Delft tiles *were discovered when this old fireplace was opened up. It had formerly been hidden behind plaster walls and was revealed only when the plaster was stripped to the brick beneath. New bricks cover the floor and the fireplace is filled with a gas log fire in an iron grate, which adds a cheerful glow to the corner of the room.*

but again did not infiltrate rural areas until well over half a century later, simply because there was no supply of electricity in many parts of the country.

The ubiquitous unit

A glass-fronted dresser top *in this carefully planned kitchen, opposite, is as decorative as it is commodious. Some of the china that it holds has a fish design, picking up the theme from the trophy catch hung on another wall (see picture above). The short curtains, roller shades or blinds and pelmets (see chapter 9) coordinate with the wallpaper and provide a fresh and cheerful background to the long refectory table and cane chairs.*

Then came the kitchen units: the wall-mounted cupboards and counter-topped base units which hid those lovely still-lives on open shelves mentioned by Mario Praz, but protected utensils from dust and grease. For a time the old country kitchen seemed to be relegated to the past in favour of hygienic laminates and stainless steel.

Happily, Terence Conran and his Habitat stores led the re-appreciation of the sturdy qualities of wood which could be scrubbed clean, of open shelves and old-fashioned dressers. Conran also produced a range of the ubiquitous units in wood, sufficiently successfully for other manufacturers to copy, thus marrying the feeling of the warm, rural kitchen with the attention to hygiene and cleanliness so prevalent in the twentieth century.

A white-painted dresser or hutch forms a visual division between the kitchen and dining parts of this large room which also undergoes a change of floors, and levels, from stripped and polished wood to white-painted boards (see chapter 9). The walls are interesting too, for they are bare but polished plaster, which makes a nice contrast to the white paint and the colourful china, as well as setting off the watercolours with their blue-grey mounts and wood frames.

The working end of the room *pictured above is shown opposite. It is neat and functional with all the* batterie de cuisine *allotted to its proper place. The lighting, too, is efficient and well placed for maximum efficiency. Nevertheless, the spirit of the lower-level eating area is caught here, with the array of copper pans, iron skillets, earthenware jugs and other more rustic kitchen accoutrements hanging from the brass rod above the saucepan rack.*

Character returns to the kitchen

Floor tiles and wall tiles have never been more plentiful. Although it is difficult to install actual flagstones, there is a good choice of bricks, quarry tiles, and square terracotta tiles, all of which give an immediate country look. If you really want the feel of flagstones, it is possible to lay ordinary concrete slabs, subsequently rubbed with shoe polish, dust and dirt and then waxed; they will give at least a good approximation of the real thing, especially if you chip them around a little (see chapter 9). The range of both revivals of old designs and of new designs in wall tiles is difficult to resist. And it is always possible to scour junk yards, demolition sites, and the now fairly numerous establishments selling architectural relics to find supplies of old pamments, bricks and tiles.

The other change for the better in kitchens is their change of venue from the furthest possible point from the living room and dining room to the nearest, since powerful extractor fans take care of smells — which in any case are a great deal less pungent than those caused by open-fire cooking — and since the lack of servants makes it imperative to site cooking and eating areas as near to each other as possible.

Currently, then, kitchens appear to have the best of both worlds: the efficiency of modern appliances and accessories and the warmth and straightforwardness of the old country models. Just because help of any sort is hard to come by, the kitchen has once again become a personal room and at the same time a more sophisticated, workable one, with no loss of the old character. Moreover, where space permits, it has also become very much a family, all-purpose room as well, with room to eat, do homework, read, or just to sit around and drink and chat. The gentrification of the kitchen has done nothing to rob it of its humble, heart of the house appeal.

CHAPTER SEVEN

BEDROOMS & CHILDREN'S ROOMS

It is gentle and venerable. It is above all an English house.

VITA SACKVILLE-WEST, *Knole and the Sackvilles*

Green and rose chintz *is a happy combination in many rural rooms. In the bedroom pictured opposite, the chintz is frilled and edged with a thin red piping and lined with a dense pink and white check, giving the room a positively euphoric glow. The painted bedhead melds in well, as do the lampshade and the dado – painted a sophisticated and quite daring red among otherwise quite gentle colouring.*

G iven the general need for privacy and, indeed, for quiet sleep, it seems extraordinary that the English bedroom did not really come into being until late in the Middle Ages and that even then it was hardly a haven, for it was one of the first outgrowths of the great hall in manor houses and castles and was generally a sort of reception room or salon as well as an actual sleeping room. At that time, and for the next few centuries, the bedroom, or chamber as it was called, was the exclusive province of the rich. Everyone else slept in the hall, in outhouses, or in hovels. And even the privileged occupiers of the chamber slept in the beginning on the floor, though occasionally mattresses, or the straw palliasses that passed for them, would be laid on cords stretched across a low, rough wooden framework to avoid the excesses of cold and damp. Furs would be used for coverings and only tapestry wallcoverings were there to allay somewhat the miserable draughts that must have whistled through the outside walls in winter.

The graceful, fretted top *of this mahogany bed is teamed with a fresh green and white cotton, lined with a similarly coloured cotton of much smaller pattern. These cottons and the fine-drawn linen of the bedclothes and pillow cases form a quiet contrast to the gentle terracotta of the walls and window drapes. Since the room is almost all bed, the background has been made to appear larger by the simple expedient of keeping the walls and ceiling the same colour and all the draperies as simple as possible.*

Entertaining in the chamber

By the fourteenth century, these primitive beds were becoming much more common, and in an effort to gain much-needed privacy from the bevy of servants and attendants who slept on straw pallets in the same room, the bed was surrounded by long curtains suspended from a canopy attached by hooks to the ceiling. Alternatively, a bed might have two posts at its foot and a solid bedhead rising high enough to support a canopy. Real four-posters did not come into being until the mid-sixteenth century, and then outer and somewhat lighter inner hangings matched valances coming from underneath the mattress to the floor. Since textiles were expensive right up to the time of mechanized spinning in the eighteenth century, such beds and their

A warm and dramatic scheme, all the more interesting for its mise en scène, in the attic room of an old farmhouse. The steeply sloping and heavily beamed ceiling is counterpointed by the sophistication of the turned, carved poles of the polished mahogany bed, just as the elaborate American "log cabin" quilt is juxtaposed with the richness of the bed and window curtains.

A spectacularly carved bed of great quality is set with striking effect between a pair of round tables with ruffled chintz tablecloths and matching lampshades. The crackle background of the chintz melds gracefully with the painted yellow-glazed walls, echoed in turn by the covering on the long, low stool. The carpet in John Fowler's favourite "mouse's-back" shade and the white covers on the high, comfortable-looking mattress are a unifying balance to the contrasting elements of elaborate carving and gracefully garlanded chintz.

hangings became major status symbols.

Elaborately carved frames and sumptuously embroidered wool hangings meant that for a time more skill and money were expended on making beds than any other item of furniture. Since they became virtually rooms within rooms and the hangings provided not only privacy but warmth, this seems logical. In any event, bed hangings were considerably more elaborate and complicated than window curtains, which did not arrive till many generations later and, when they did, were much simpler affairs without valance or pelmet, and rarely divided into pairs until the eighteenth century. Indeed many windows were altogether curtainless until that time, and their owners made do with shutters.

An ornate state bed *with hangings and bedhead of great sophistication is set on a rush mat floor in a time-honoured way and enhanced by the subtle glazing and colouring of the panelled walls. The exquisitely figured table at the end of the bed is topped by a silver dressing-table set and the other handsome table in front of the window holds a fine collection of china. Dark velvet curtains, edged with red, tone with the different fabric of the bedspread but do not match it. Note also how the motif on the curtain pelmet repeats, but does not entirely copy, the motif on the elaborate bed pelmets and how the gilt candle sconces have much the same feeling as the picture frame to the left of the window.*

A composition in greens *is here almost a competition of greens. Stippled green walls (see chapter 9) match the glazed top of the painted dressing table, which in turn goes with the marbled chair. The terracotta of the chair seat is reflected in the decoration of the dressing table.*

Diversely covered and shaped *pillows give a nicely relaxed look and contrast interestingly with the traditional candlewick design of the bed cover, overprinted, less traditionally, with a random red leaf design.*

It is hardly surprising, then, that such elaborate beds should be used as the framework for the lady of the house, who often lay on her mattress, fully dressed and immaculately coiffed, to receive her guests. This was not nearly so odd as it seems, given that the "chamber" was still used as a form of family living room for informal receptions, card parties, small supper parties and so on. However, when the bed was not in use as a day bed for "receptions", the curtains surrounding it were kept closed since the sight of the bedclothes could be construed as unseemly. By the 1660s, grand houses generally had one "apartment" for a husband and another for his wife. An apartment meant personal living quarters as opposed to reception areas, and ranged from a single bedchamber with closets off it to a whole string of rooms.

Ornate iron and brass bedsteads *were very much a part of the English country bedroom from the mid-nineteenth century and through the Edwardian era. This one, in a child's bedroom in an old farmhouse, provides a down to earth balance, as well as sleeping space, for the cloud-cuckoo-land wallpaper and the roseate colours of the patchwork quilt. The sharp angle of the ceiling is outlined by the beams, which make a strong counterpoint to the thin black iron curves of the bedstead.*

The detail views of the bed, *above and left, show the nice intricacies of the ironwork, the effective juxtaposition of the black curves with the square frame of the sampler above the bed head, and the* insouciant *mix of wallpaper and curtains.*

Dais and balustrade from France

In the seventeenth century, English decoration, like that of the rest of Europe, was deeply influenced by the French, and the sleeping chamber in particular became very richly furnished as well as bedded. During the reign of Louis XIV, the French introduced the practice of raising the bed on a dais separated from the rest of the room by columns and a balustrade. This gave rise to the more general habit of dividing the decoration of the room into two parts: the walls in the sitting part of the room being panelled and painted, while those of the "sleeping alcove", as it was often called, were hung with tapestries or velvet or some other rich material, like embroidered wool or crewel work, in keeping with the elaborate hangings that surrounded the bed. At this period, the bed hangings were used as much to keep the heat in, as to ward off any possibility of an unwelcome ration of air, which in those days was considered eminently unwholesome. It probably was, given the lack of running water for washing, the general paucity of elementary hygiene, and the fact that the toilet was generally a

An exotic painted bench makes a fanciful addition to an otherwise rather chaste little four-poster bed with its creamy hangings and canopy and spanking white bed covering. The pale terracotta of the painted walls looks good with the colours of the rug and against the crisp white painted woodwork. The final effect is unexpected but memorable.

Solemn plaster profiles *of Queen Victoria and Prince Albert surmount this padded bedhead covered in Laura Ashley cotton. The walls behind are covered with the same cotton, hung curtain-like from a brass pole suspended all the way around the room – an excellent way to disguise less than perfect plaster (see wall treatments, chapter 9). Although pillows are covered in similar Laura Ashley cottons, the bedspread itself is Indian.*

A handsome mahogany bed *with an Edwardian lace bedspread has the kind of half-tester recommended in the nineteenth century as better for the health since lots of draperies were thought to be too stuffy. The creamy cotton lining matching the valance or bed ruffle looks clean and simple against the red and cream cotton and the carpet with its oriental rug. Note the subtle detailing, such as the edging on the canopy and the thin red border running all round the room just below the cornice and just above the dado.*

chaise percée, or closed-chair, sometimes placed right in the bedroom itself.

Privacy in the eighteenth century

As long as the chamber continued to be a general receiving room or salon it was decorated with a good deal of elaboration, but by the eighteenth century it was becoming an altogether more private affair leading off the withdrawing room on the ground floor or *piano nobile*. The plan of large country houses of the time was analogous to a tunnel with the main reception rooms at the open end and the more private bedrooms, studies, closets, dressing rooms and so on at the other. Thus privacy really was assured because servants could fend off unwelcome visitors and, in any case, people were able to make discreet exits through doors in the series of little rooms leading off the main bedroom.

Although bedrooms in grand country houses remained elaborate, they were considerably more simple than they had been in the

This spacious bedroom, *opposite, overlooking a dense mass of trees, is large enough to have a comfortable sitting area, making it like a nineteenth-century boudoir or elegant receiving room. Red and white double doors make a dramatic entry and the stunning juxtaposition of the gentle chintz with the stippled scarlet walls (see chapter 9) and thin scarlet trim to the ruffles is as effective as the quieter mixture of upholstery fabrics set on the pale carpet. The memorabilia crowding the papier mâché tray table add welcoming personal touches.*

preceding century. Very often the rather grand alcove containing the bed became more of a niche in the wall of a much smaller space. Elaborate tapestries and hangings gave way to plain wood panelling, and the heavy carved ceilings to light plaster traceries. But the biggest change was brought about by the import of cottons and linens from the Far East which triggered the taste for simpler fabrics; and as well as these imported "Indiennes", people began to use plain white linens, feather mattresses, and thin, washable, unlined cottons for window and bed curtains. This was in keeping with the introduction of new ideas of hygiene – and not before time.

The humble bedroom

Nor were bedrooms any longer the exclusive property of the rich. If the eighteenth century was the golden age of the large country house, it was also a golden age for building in general; farmhouses, rectories, lodges, village houses and cottages were springing up all over the country. By the Regency period, not only were bedrooms much

Stone-framed windows *match the simple stone surround of the fireplace at one end of a large, comfortable bedroom in a seventeenth-century house. The calm pale terracotta of the walls ties in with the chintz behind the deep-seated sofa with its lace throw, and the room is given an extravagant feel by the table lavished with satin and embroidered lace and displaying a highly unexpected (given the sumptuous fabrics) collection of ceramic owls.*

The French fashion *for placing beds long side on to the wall was recommended in England in the nineteenth century as a good position for young girls. Here, an elaborate canopy has been formed by draping the glazed plain chintz over a brass pole fixed to the wall and catching it back with old brass pins. The border pasted just below the ceiling matches the bed cover and makes an effective framework for the plain painted walls, while the varying yellows juxtaposed with the white woodwork give the room an interesting tonality.*

smaller, simpler and cleaner, but chairs and sofas were upholstered with removable slip covers in checked, striped or plain cotton; and painted panelling, bare brick, or polished or painted wide floorboards were kept deliberately unadorned save for the odd oriental or embroidered rug or piece of Brussels carpet. As Oliver Goldsmith wrote of a humbler bedroom:

"The white-wash'd wall, the nicely sanded floor,
The varnish'd clock that click'd behind the door,
The chest contriv'd a double debt to pay,
A bed at night, a chest of drawers by day."

Muslins and cottons were used for light curtains and bed coverings by both the rich and the middle classes, together with the occasional new embroidered silks from China. Indeed the printed cotton copies of these silks, which became more and more Europeanized and floral in motif as time wore on, devolved into the flowery chintzes of the nineteenth century. Thus colours became much clearer and lighter. Indeed, bedrooms were lighter because they had once again moved upstairs.

Simple sprigged wallpaper *by Laura Ashley makes an effortlessly charming background for the strong lines of the old washstand with its painted marble top and gilded decoration, and the pretty nineteenth-century chair with a seat to match the curtains, which, of course, coordinate happily with the walls. The ivy-framed oval mirror works equally well with the old ewer and basin set beneath it.*

An elegant old chintz *in the best English tradition makes a handsome bedhanging for this nineteenth-century mahogany bed. Together with the patchwork quilt, it provides a cool foil for the various reds on walls, curtains and couch, and, of course, the William Morris cushions. The* papier mâché *chair has the suitably battered seat that is endemic to at least one room in an English country house, which, above all things, should not look newly done. Simple matting on the floor sets off the decoration of the furniture.*

Bedroom suites

Richer people retained their boudoirs and dressing rooms as part of the bedroom suite, a comfortable habit that was to remain. The bathroom also was introduced in the nineteenth century, instead of the tin bath set before the bedroom fire, as another adjunct with bath, basin and so on installed in a former bedroom or dressing room.

In these suites, the boudoir customarily contained a writing table, *chaise longue* or day bed, and one or two comfortable armchairs. The well-appointed dressing room included a bed, toilet and dressing table, washstand, clothes press, cheval mirror, armchair and perhaps a desk, one or two chests of drawers and a large wardrobe. The bedroom itself offered just a bed and its accessories like bedside tables, a couple of chairs and perhaps another *chaise* at the foot of the bed. Interestingly, matching pairs of bedside tables, or night tables as they were called then, were a comparatively new invention. Few English bedrooms had them before 1760. Prior to that it was customary to have a chair beside the bed rather than any sort of table. Robert Kerr in *The*

159

Subtly shaded dragged woodwork *on a panelled door is enhanced by the handsome brass door handle and keys.*

A truly British bedroom *in a truly British house . . . this spacious room has* toile de Jouey *wallpaper, wonderful windows and distinguished furniture. A mahogany sofa table, in front of the left window, is used as a dressing table, and the mirror-fronted bureau bookcase makes a splendidly capacious bedroom desk.*

Gentleman's House (1864) talks of the "head of the bed being to the wall after the English manner" as opposed to the French – and the Italian – habit of placing one side of the bed to the wall or in an alcove, which, Kerr opined, was an idea worth copying for young ladies.

Beds were often dressed in the same way as windows in particularly fashionable bedrooms, for, in the nineteenth century, most curtains were divided and looped back "rather low than high", as the Arrowsmiths declared in their *The Housepainters and Decorators' Guide* (1840), and draped gracefully over the floor, rather than being of the pull-up and festoon variety so popular from the late seventeenth century to the late eighteenth and now, of course, popular again. The alternative window style current during the first thirty years or so of

English rose wallpaper *tones with an interesting glazed chintz in miniscule checks with a reverse trim and lining – a Regency idea. The writing desk is in a good position in front of the window for a contemplative rural view and on it stand a pair of small marble obelisks which add another Regency touch to the room.*

the century was to throw lengths of drapery over a brass or wooden pole with elaborate finials. This drapery was generally of silk or fine wool with a contrast lining for effect. Underneath was a much lighter curtain of muslin or lace, which was supposed both to keep out insects when the window was open and to soften the erratic sunlight.

"Austrian" or festoon blinds made of net remained popular under sets of curtains long after the curtains themselves had become simpler. In 1919, the American writers Eberlein, McClure and Holloway, who also worked from London, wrote: "The most sensible treatment for the usual double-sash window is that of simple curtains of white or ivory white on rings, suspended on a simple brass rod." There was some controversy over Venetian blinds. Rhoda and Agnes Garrett in their *Suggestions for Home Decorating* (1876) wrote scornfully about the "everlasting drab or yellow Venetian blinds which are constantly out of order, and always draw up crooked". Others, however, were enthusiastic, pointing out that such blinds could be painted any tint to go with their surroundings. Roller blinds were also common at the end of the nineteenth century. They were mostly made of holland, a fabric much used for such blinds, usually in off-white, occasionally red, and sometimes striped or with scalloped borders along their lower edges.

Painted roller blinds or shades were also fashionable for most years of the century. According to Peter Thornton in *Authentic Decor*, there was a book by an Edward Orme, published as far back as 1807 and called *Essay in Transparent Prints*, which gave details on how to decorate blinds of silk, linen or wire gauze with oil paints and varnish. But they were also popular in woven fabrics or plain Holland with a trim of fringe or lace.

A theme of early spring, *with thick bunches of daffodils inside the window echoing those outside, even the cachepot has a daffodil design and the varying yellows in the curtain fabric, china, books and in the twisted rope of the tie-backs all contribute to the freshness of the scene. The old polished oak writing table and mirror make an effective counterpoint to the exquisite early spring view outside.*

La vie en rouge *with a bonus of roses in another elaborately curtained bedroom with a very grand lambrequin-like canopy over the beds. The rose prints in different scales for duvets and tablecloth are in unexpected contrast to the ribbon print with its dashing red bows. The pale lining tones well with the wallpaper and the red ceramic lamp.*

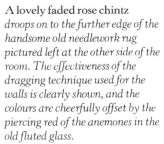

A lovely faded rose chintz *droops on to the further edge of the handsome old needlework rug pictured left at the other side of the room. The effectiveness of the dragging technique used for the walls is clearly shown, and the colours are cheerfully offset by the piercing red of the anemones in the old fluted glass.*

Simple coia matting *forms a quiet, sober background for all the detail in this richly furnished room. The panelled walls have been dragged (see chapter 9) in two striking shades of pink finely edged with subtly tinted white. The distinguished colouring of the elaborate needlework rug is reflected in the dark shade of the skirting or baseboards and in the needlework cushion on the bed. Rosy chintz used for the bedhead and valance is effectively offset by the mahogany-red throw and the lighter red shades of the pillows and tablecloth.*

Less formal beds

The word bedroom did not become current until the mid-nineteenth century as chambers gradually fell into disuse. By then muslins and damasks and dimity cottons were popular for bedrooms in smaller country houses and farms, while lace, the favourite of the Edwardians, began to be used by the upper classes. Wooden beds gave way to painted cast iron and brass, and Cassell's *Household Guide* stated that "medical men consider it the more healthy plan to sleep on beds with as few draperies as possible". They suggested the half-tester as a good compromise, with curtains that hung down from a canopy attached to ceiling or wall, according to ceiling height, and projecting about half a yard (45cm) over the pillow area. "Such beds," it said, "admit of curtains without entirely eradicating the air." This was probably the start of the British fresh air fetish which was to reach its apotheosis in the 1920s and 1930s when belief in the virtues of country air led to a passion for open windows and for, as Mark Girouard put it in *Life in the English Country House*, "living, working, eating and sleeping in or

163

164

A rather grand chintz *in this handsome guest room has been used as a starting point for a collection of interesting details. The gathered pelmets with their deep scallops have been edged with plain red, as have the leading edges of the curtains at window and bed, and the bed ruffle or valance. Note the much thinner, subtle red banding that delineates the top section of both sets of curtains. Matching bed and window treatments were very fashionable in the mid-nineteenth century and have hardly fallen from grace since. The curtains are lined with a simple cotton to match the wallpaper, which itself is bordered just below the cornice. The pristine embroidered linen tablecloth looks well with the handsome sheets and blanket cover, and even the porcelain bowl seems to match.*

Apple blossom and fresh green *fabric with a delicate faded air is used here for seductively comfortable quilted eiderdowns or comforters, as well as for the interestingly pelmeted curtains and the bed draperies with their somewhat dégagé tie-backs. Palest blossom pink walls and the green patterned bedheads add to the spring orchard feeling, with the green serendipitously repeating the exact colour of the leaves outside the window. A flowered border gives gentle delineation to the generally delicate room.*

Low, steeply sloping ceilings *are very much a part of bedrooms in old farmhouses and cottages, for they are often tucked away under the eaves. Here, a comfortable looking bed is neatly fitted under just such a beamed ceiling, although the beams have been painted in with the uneven plaster (which is again endemic to such houses).*

above the garden" in sleeping porches or on bedroom balconies. In any case, beds took on a less formal air. They might have no hangings at all or, if they did, they would be simple and of light materials – lace, muslin, chintz or gingham. These would perhaps be teamed with lace bed covers or old quilted cotton or patchwork quilts that provided colour and comfort.

Pretty clutter

The late nineteenth century was the time of the accessory: the stuffed birds in glass cases or under glass domes; the bird's eye maple frames for samplers, prints, small watercolours, engravings and oleographs; the china jugs, vases and figures; the busts, and phrenologists' heads;

Fresh blue and white curtains *are draped around a particularly handsome bed, their dense design contrasting nicely with the simplicity of the wallpaper. The oak chest at the foot of the bed provides a useful surface for magazines, books and objects as well as an effective stand for a generous basket of hydrangeas. The carpet is the inconspicuous shade of grey-fawn that the late John Fowler referred to as "mouse's back".*

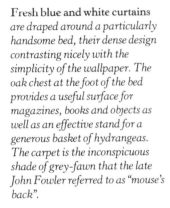

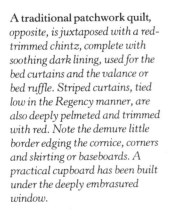

A traditional patchwork quilt, *opposite, is juxtaposed with a red-trimmed chintz, complete with soothing dark lining, used for the bed curtains and the valance or bed ruffle. Striped curtains, tied low in the Regency manner, are also deeply pelmeted and trimmed with red. Note the demure little border edging the cornice, corners and skirting or baseboards. A practical cupboard has been built under the deeply embrasured window.*

the painted washstands, occasional tables and attractively framed mirrors. Most rooms still had fireplaces with pretty little mantelpieces and grates, embroidered rugs, or Brussels or Axminster carpets, sometimes patterned or bordered, and almost always with a surround of bare boards which could be painted, marbled, stencilled or stained.

Walls were often papered with the fresh sprigged flower designs that are still a hallmark of rural English rooms, or with William Morris designs, or the Art Nouveau designs of Walter Crane, Charles Voysey or Arthur H. Mackmurdo, for the wallpaper business was booming in England. Stencilling, which repeated patterns for borders or corner ornamentation on walls and ceilings, was also enormously popular.

The contemporary country bedroom
It is this sort of gentle eclecticism that has evolved into the comfortable country bedroom of today: a room that might well have a painted

White and blue wallpaper *and matching Laura Ashley curtains are teamed with a much more complicated design of Persian intensity for the mattress cover, valance, bedhead and bolster, which fits well with the Brussels rug. Note the nonchalant tie of the curtain at the foot of the bed. The plethora of pillows in differing shapes and sizes betrays a dressing-room bed used more for casual lounging than for serious sleeping.*

An oak leaf and acorn stencil *borders the fireplace and chair rail of this room and cleverly repeats in more fluid form the oak leaf design in the actual mantelpiece. The shelf holds a formidable profusion of objects and memorabilia massed as tightly together as the leaves and acorns below.*

A very splendid bedhead *is the immediate focal point of this bedroom but the eye is then drawn to all the other fetching details: the deep border panelling the walls; the interesting way that the collection of sludgy-green-mounted drawings are hung either side of the bed; the stencilled linen of curtains and sofa cover; the chaste and faded design on the bed cover repeated in the tablecloth on the bedside table and the rose in it again picked up in the old ruffled pillow on the armchair. The matting on the floor is softened by various rugs, and the capacious double chest of drawers or bureau makes a practical bed end.*

169

floor, gingham bed drapes on an old white-painted or brass bed, white shutters, a light cloth and over-cloth flung over at least one round table, a desk and bedside tables piled with books and bottles of Malvern water, and gently billowing curtains over a charming blind, just the sort of bedroom in fact that was imported into America in the nineteenth century to become part of an indigenous American country style as well.

But equally, an English country bedroom might have a much more ancient four poster, or a bed with a half tester, and it might have comfortable carpeting topped with a *gros point* rug in front of a gently glowing fire. It could have long glazed chintz curtains and blinds, or festoon blinds (with their roots in the eighteenth century), or pull-up

An unusually shaped window *set in the thick wall of an old stone farmhouse makes a natural display space. Here, the deep emerald shade of the blind sets off the soft tawny-greens and blue of the landscape, and the varying greens and blues of the glass collection.*

Battered stuffed toys *that have clearly seen a lot of love along with better days are firmly wedged into a bowl and make a charming group in front of this open window, framed by the sophisticated chintz of the curtains and backed by the garden view. All seems well with the world. . . .*

curtains, or simply short cotton curtains in the case, perhaps, of a cottage with tiny windows. It could have any of these things, all elements drawn from various centuries, but the main characteristic of the comfortable English bedroom is an unforced elegance slightly coming apart at the seams, a room full of memorabilia, the kind of room that the late Christian Dior labelled a "Nanny" room; a room that is not at all grand, a room that has "happened" rather than a room that has been decorated.

Nurseries and childrens' rooms

"Nanny" rooms, of course, make one think of nurseries and children's rooms steeped in nostalgia. These again owe more to the late

Scarlet is the theme in this white-plastered old farmhouse room with its Edwardian brass beds and rockers. The rag rug looks quite at home with the unaffected mixture of contemporary paintings and comfortable Edwardiana, and the plant in the exceptionally deep window embrasure is nicely set against the scarlet draperies or curtains.

eighteenth and the nineteenth centuries than to earlier times. Before the Victorian age, children hardly entered into the planning of a house; they were just fitted in wherever it seemed convenient. But the Victorian concept of a large united family meant that children were placed within easy reach of their parents, sometimes on the floor above the parents' rooms, to enable doting mothers to run up to see their offspring. There is a charming recollection of Marjorie Strachey's in *Two Victorian Families* by Betty Askwith: "Mama used to wear a little gold bell on her watch chain. The nursery was right at the top of a very high house, and the inhabitants were apt to feel lonely and cut off from the rest of the world. Suddenly one would hear the tinkling of the gold bell coming nearer and nearer. I shall never forget the exciting

anticipation of interest and pleasure that came with it."

Most nurseries, then, are firmly entrenched in Victoriana or Edwardiana: the club fender around the fire, the old rocking chair, the white-painted iron crib, the battered cots and base or skirting boards, wallpaper shredded here and there, and books and toys going back generations, comforting each in turn. There will be a battered chesterfield with some of the stuffing oozing out. The floor will either be bare polished boards or linoleum with theadbare rugs – paying scant attention to all thoughts of slipping and tumbling – or it will be somewhat battered vinyl or cork. Windows will be barred up to a sensible height unless the room is on the ground floor, and there will inevitably be a gate at the top of the stairs.

And scarlet again *in this equally bold, primary colour scheme for a child's bedroom in another old house. The red of the painted floor (see chapter 9) is continued round the edges of the blackboards which cunningly cover the closet doors. The footprint frieze above the alphabet adds a nice touch of whimsey, as do the painted birds on the white chest of drawers.*

A well-protected fire *in the grate, a dog lying on the shaggy hearthrug, a rocking horse, a doll's house and a couple of shapeless comfortable chairs, what else could one possibly need in a proper English country house nursery? Well, good storage, of course, and that is provided in this room pictured opposite by a capacious chest of drawers and closets, apart from the useful two-tiered table on which the doll's house sits and (outside the picture) long low bookshelves. Other nice nostalgic touches are the bellows and hobby horse, the array of Victorian postcards over the mantelshelf and the old prints. The brown pileless carpet defies stains as well as being hard enough to run toys over, yet soft enough to sit and crawl on, and the white walls will absorb any amount of other colour as the years progress. Now they show up the alphabet frieze that runs round the room underneath the cornice.*

Young children's bedrooms *were not taken into the general planning of grand country houses until the nineteenth century. Before that, they were fitted in wherever was deemed most practical, as indeed was the case in most houses whatever the income level. From the mid-1900s, however, there was a radical change. Here, a pretty child's bed – of the kind that one could imagine Frances Hodgson Burnett, that romantic Victorian writer of children's tales, would think her* Little Princess *would deserve at the end of all her travails – is charmingly curtained with a diminutive floral crisply edged with green. In similar vein, the cane bedhead has been bordered with the same fabric but edged in rose pink. The old-fashioned eiderdown is also covered in the floral fabric and given a miniscule frill. The lavish attention to detail adds up to a charming whole.*

Walls will probably be white or a plain, light colour, but there might well be a dado round the room covered with transfers like a Victorian patch screen, or with old magazine cuttings, all carefully layered with varnish to make it easily washable as much as to preserve it for posterity. There might also be some old prints with light-hearted animal themes or samplers of previous generations' early attempts at needlework.

As Rupert Brooke wrote in that most English of poems *The Old Vicarage, Grantchester*:

". . . Oh! yet
Stands the church clock at ten to three?
And is there honey still for tea?"

CHAPTER EIGHT

BATHROOMS

. . . a chain you could pull which brought water pouring down . . .
Laura had not seen this marvel.

FLORA THOMPSON, *Lark Rise to Candleford*

An elaborately soft frame *is made for this old village church, opposite, by the print curtains and the ruffled Austrian blind or shade. Even if the window treatment was removed, the simple blue and white tiles used to line both bath panel and walls would still make an interesting frame for the ecclesiastical view. The deep peach rag-rubbed effect paper on the doors (by Osborne & Little, who have saved many a hard-working day with the glaze and the rags – see chapter 9) picks up the tawny highlights that enrich the church stonework.*

ritish bathrooms have not, on the whole, been conspicuous for their comfort, their decoration, or, unlike other rooms, their steady improvement over the years. And they have rarely had any of the seductive, even erotic, connotations of some of their European counterparts. The chief interest of the British bathroom, in fact, lies in its extraordinarily chequered career: in favour, out of favour, used as a meeting place for both sexes, segregated, neglected, resurrected for relaxation, used only for quick cleansing, a place middle-class Victorians would sidle into. It has emerged, been perfected, submerged and emerged again with a quite alarming disregard for cleanliness and sanitation.

A thousand years of squalor
An Englishman complained of his Oxford college in the 1950s that it denied him the everyday conveniences of Minoan Crete. And indeed, Minoan skill in sanitary engineering appears to have far surpassed that

Comfortable mahogany
commodes were a feature of the nineteenth century and are often used now in country homes to surround a more conventional modern water closet. Here, the deep tones of the mahogany are picked up by the choice of wallpaper and bird-patterned chintz.

177

Highly decorated bowls *were another feature of Victorian times, whether for wash basins or W.C.s. This one, nicely sunk into a polished and panelled bench, is somewhat reminiscent of the W.C. in a comfortable turn-of-the-century train. The red-painted wash basin pipe is a decorative touch.*

of the Chaldeans, the Egyptians and the Greeks who were all, in turn, far superior to the Anglo-Saxons who had hardly a bathroom to call their own until the late seventeenth century. The Queen's bathroom in King Minos' palace at Knossos, unearthed by Sir Arthur Evans in the early part of this century, was as sumptuous a room as any contemporary luxurious bathroom. It included an ergonomically satisfying and beautifully decorated bath, good for all its thousands of years. Even the water closets were curiously modern. One of them evidently had a wooden seat and probably an earthenware pan, as well as a reservoir for flushing water.

Although not quite so talented at plumbing, the ancient Greeks by all accounts, and in particular Homer's, at least always had good hot baths to return to after their interminable travels. And according to *Clean and Decent*, Lawrence Wright's invaluable history of the bath, fourth-century Rome had 11 public baths, 1352 fountains and cisterns and 856 private baths. Some private houses in Pompeii are believed to have had as many as 30 taps, and, as well as private water-flushing latrines, there were plenty of public ones. Rome, for example, had 144, and, at its peak, supplied 300 gallons of water per head a day. (In London now, not much more than 51 gallons per head a day are used, of which 34 are for domestic and 17 for public use.)

I mention these facts more from a sense of irony than of history; for the British, who so pride themselves on their civilized ways, have one of the least clean records in Europe. It is a salutary thought that the Roman occupation of Britain lasted well over 300 years, during which the Romans built a sophisticated network of public baths, plumbing systems and aqueducts, and were known to have many private baths as well. Yet, when they left, almost every one of their civilized customs and habits was effaced within a frighteningly short

Another throne-like commode, *opposite, is set in an alcove on a step up from the rest of the bathroom. The red-brown richness of the mahogany is given full rein against the discreet beige wallpaper and the soft beige carpet. Piles of books and banks of prints complete the comfortable air.*

An interesting quatrefoil *window forms a distinguished endpiece to a handsome bathroom with a dado and cornice of carved wood and a centrally placed bath with a wide marble surround – all the better to put things on. The room is beautifully detailed: note, for example, the brass grille set into the top of the chair rail which lets out hot air. And how very nice to relax in a foamy bath and have that sort of rural view to contemplate. Wallpaper in a bathroom can be covered with a coat of either matt or semi-gloss polyurethane (first testing on a small corner to make sure the colour does not run) to give it a nice sheen, take away the newness and, best of all, make it washable.*

time. For almost a thousand years after the Roman legions marched away there was hardly a tap to turn in Britain, let alone anything as sophisticated as a water closet.

High standards in monasteries

Although it was more normal to go largely unwashed for centuries after this, there was a major exception: medieval monasteries set a shining example of cleanliness. At Canterbury in Kent, a complete water service was installed in the monastery in 1150. It must have been efficient: that particular monastery was one of few communities to escape the Black Death in 1349. A stream for drainage was important for the site of monastery; and many of the "romantic" secret passages that seem clandestinely to have linked monasteries with convents are much more likely to have been chaste but practical sewers. Water flushing was rare, but the Abbot of St. Alban's in Hertfordshire built a stone cistern to catch rainwater to serve his "necessary" house – the medieval latrine. Many ruined monasteries

A nice old-fashioned bath *with rather more modern taps or faucets is sited beneath another round window, this time of the oeil de boeuf variety and treated with a chintz festoon shade or blind which looks effective up or down. That very English thing, a heated towel rail, can be seen near the tap end of the bath. These civilized appliances are often in evidence in English bathrooms, but are rarely seen in America, the birthplace of modern creature comforts. A constant supply of warm towels, one would think, would be a necessity in any sybaritic bathing room.*

181

ENGLISH COUNTRY STYLE

Bedrooms turned into *bathrooms produce nice spacious rooms with a leisurely air about them, a far cry from the clinical little tiled cells in so many city flats or apartments. Here, the original old bath has been kept but a marble wash basin has been sunk into a nineteenth-century night table and skilfully plumbed into the wall. Festoon blinds form their own pelmets above filmy lace curtains, and an oriental rug on top of the neutral carpet adds another touch of richness to the room.*

display sociable rows of pierced stone seats, sometimes back to back, with a small division between each, though occasionally they were arranged in a circle. Their bath houses had plain round or oval wooden tubs, made of oak or walnut.

Social bathing

Less holy citizens were not so punctilious. Medieval books of etiquette insisted upon the washing of hands, face and teeth every morning, and the washing of hands before and after meals (only practical, one supposes, since people ate with their fingers); but they made no particular mention of bathing, though baths certainly existed and were at least offered to travellers when they first arrived. Their shape was similar to that of contemporary baths, but they were mostly built to allow several people to bathe at once. Hot water was scarce, since there were no pipes, so whole families and their guests would bathe together, which was presumably more sociable than sanitary, and carouse together too. There is a fascinating late fifteenth-century

Conventional bath-time objects *like ducks and shells are markedly present in this room, yet they are not so very conventional. The duck, for instance, is skilfully wrought in cane and bears a tiny duckling on its back. The shells are esoteric and are displayed not only by the bath but on the shelf of the handsome white and gilt mirror above the end of the bath, along with unusual china birds. The somewhat eclectic prints, too, are interesting and all of these elements together with the warm apricot walls and the honey-toned marble surround to the bath make for an interesting room to soak in.*

Curtains are matched to bath *panel in this thoroughly rural bathroom (another detail is on p. 195) with its strong pattern of beams against nicely battered plaster. The bath, with its practical wide surround, has been fitted in very sympathetically to what must have been a bedroom in former days. Now, the linking device of the same design for fabric and plastic laminate makes a particularly fresh and pretty statement. Note,* too, *the single bow attached to the deep fabric pelmet above the curtains.*

A blue and white basin like a Chinese willow pattern plate looks particularly good embedded in this marble-topped mahogany unit. Brass taps or faucets complete the effect of quality, helped by the blue and white bowl full of soaps and the blue bottle — and the shafts of sunlight through the window.

woodcut showing a bath house cum bordello where a minstrel plays to couples seated either side of a long wooden bath with a centreboard full of food, plates and mugs, while a man "washes" a woman's legs at the far end. There are other pictures of smaller, more familial tubs, also with an eating board across and invariably with mixed occupants. There were evidently no inhibitions about men and women bathing together. If everyone slept huggermugger, they could certainly take the occasional bath together too. Some more important people had baths to themselves. Certainly, King John was said to have taken a bath in a wooden tub about once every three weeks, and restorations of medieval castles show similar wooden, portable tubs that were designed for one person.

In these great houses, such tubs would be brought into the private sleeping quarters and filled with hot water. Very often they were padded with linen cloths and provided with a wooden stool to shield the occupant from the rough, clammy sides. Sometimes too, the entire bath was enveloped in a tent of fabric, more for the steam this

Dark duck-patterned tiles *make a strong twentieth-century background for this converted nineteenth-century basin resting on an old wash stand with plumbing cleverly concealed behind. Note the decorative touches of the large porcelain swan crouched beneath the basin stand and its small counterpart above, and the second basin exotically filled with flowers.*

engendered than the privacy. In the fifteenth century, a few royal palaces actually had fixed baths, properly cased in, with, in rare instances, a crude system of running water, but there was still nothing resembling the ancient classical comforts.

"The necessary"

W.C.s, or what passed for them, were called "necessariums", "the necessary", or the "garderobe" – a forerunner of the cloakroom. Great houses and castles usually possessed such garderobes within the thickness of their walls, each with its own vertical shaft below the stone or wooden seat. And, just as the myth of the connecting passages between monasteries and nunneries can be explained away by sewers, so many of the so-called "priest's hiding holes" in old houses may well have been the latrines.

For the rest of the population, there were a few private "necessaries" for the rich, more public ones for the less fortunate, and the ubiquitous chamber pot. Public baths regained a certain amount of

A fully panelled bathroom, *especially one with a fireplace, is the stuff that dreams are made of, and this room is exceptionally handsome. The window at the bath end of the room gives an indication of the room's impressive height, and the brown marbled tiles of the bath panel and surround look good against the woodwork. A light touch is added by the two French prints above the taps, "Les différentes positions sociales de l'homme", providing subjects for rueful contemplation in the bath.*

favour via Turkey, when the returning crusaders reported on the merits of such facilities.

While the sixteenth-century Italian popes and nobles had sumptuous bathrooms with frescoed walls, marble baths, and hot and cold water taps; and while Leonardo da Vinci was devising hot water systems providing pre-mixed bathwater, three parts hot and one part cold, and water closets with flushing channels and ventilating shafts; the British made no sanitary progress at all, save for the portable necessaries, called "close-stools" or "stools of ease", kept in their sleeping quarters, or just outside. These were box-like stools with padded seats, often made of pleasant-smelling cedar wood, and sometimes decorated with velvet, leather, or elaborate painting.

The flush W.C.

In the 1590s, a century after Leonardo da Vinci, Sir John Harrington, a godson of Elizabeth I, designed a water closet complete with seat, pan, cistern, overflow pipe, flushing system, valve and a waste with a water

The black marble fire surround *is shown up well by the black toilet seat at the other side of the panelled bathroom, and by the black mounts of the blown-up photographs on the wall - which also bring a modern element to the room. Note how the pipes to the tank above the lavatory and the tank itself have been painted in with the walls for greater subtlety.*

seal. But, although the Queen had one built in her palace at Richmond (she already had a bathing room at Windsor Castle, wainscoted in glass, to which she repaired once a month), the invention did not come into general use until it was reinvented some two hundred years later.

In the seventeenth century, even Samuel Pepys, that enormously civilized man, kept a "close-stool" in his dining room, and in country towns all over the British Isles the contents of these "close-stools" were tipped out of countless upstairs windows onto the streets below to the accompaniment of warning cries of "Gardy-loo", derived, in the Anglo-French cross culture, from "Gardez l'eau" (mind the water). In large country houses these closed stools were generally installed in separate closets off the bedchamber, and servants removed the contents more discreetly. In lesser houses people simply made do with pots under the bed. In France superior versions of the closed stool that could be flushed were called "Lieux à L'Anglais" (English places), the derivation of the modern English "loo". However, most travelled Frenchmen denied actually having seen such a thing in England.

Honeysuckled trellis paper and a charming nineteenth-century fireplace in the corner make a pretty background for this room with its idiosyncratic painted and gilded mirror, its fern obelisks and its early print. The wallpapered panel at the front of the bath and the ledge at the end are covered with sheets of glass for protection, as are the walls surrounding the bath. Note the ubiquitous heated towel rail to the side.

189

The deep mirrored archway in which this bath is set makes the room appear to stretch on and on. But even without the reflections, the room is singularly stylish with its two long windows, its judiciously placed green paint, its flamestitch curtains, and its table draped in green cloth by the white-painted commode (all reflected in the mirror). This concept of the visual double arch — the repetitive arched mirror gives that illusion — is an excellent idea for a long narrow room. The colours too are fresh and interesting, and the room is given a particularly personal note by the montage of family photographs.

Paper and fabric are matched *in this small farmhouse bathroom with its deeply beamed and sloping ceiling. To stop the beams from becoming too dominant, they have mostly been painted in with the plaster, and the decorative device of keeping fabric and paper the same has unified the other surfaces in as cohesive a way as possible in a necessarily fragmented space, for rooms under the eaves are invariably full of little bits and pieces of wall and usurping ceiling.*

Nonetheless, ten W.C.s were installed in the Duke of Devonshire's Chatsworth in the early 1690s. They were made of cedar with brass fittings, and a few baths of alabaster or marble were introduced as well. In lesser houses, the servants brought in copper baths and placed them in front of the bedchamber fire. In farms and small country houses this ritual was more likely to take place in front of the kitchen range.

The rise of the bathroom

During the eighteenth century, bathrooms in large country houses became more common with the addition of plunge baths and primitive showers. In 1730 the Duke of Marlborough had his own bathroom at Blenheim placed outside his library for all to see with bowl, tub, floors and walls in marble, a Japanned seat and a W.C. At Woburn, in 1748, the Duke of Bedford installed a drainage system, complete with four water closets, "at least one within the house". Isaac Ware's *A Complete Body of Architecture* (1756) shows external "bog-houses" to a very large house, but none at all indoors. The architect James Paine put a single water closet into the huge Kedleston Hall; and Osterley House, in the same period, had one sidled into a niche in a room with a door so close to the seat as to hide it only when it was not in use. Even in 1760 fixed water closets were very rare indeed. Horace Walpole, writing of Aelia Laelia Chudley's house, says: "But of all curiosities, are the *conveniences* in every bedchamber: great mahogany projections . . . with the holes, with brass handles, and cocks, &c. – I

Nicely drawn, nicely faded *chintz trailing leisurely on the ground makes this bathroom with its deep window ledge and shutters, and its matching pine skirting or baseboards look comfortably and elegantly rural. The rose edging on the pelmets finishes them neatly, and they have also been given rather skittish (for a bathroom) trumpet headings. The beige-patterned wallpaper echoes the design of the panels in the chintz and is effective against the blocks of waxed pine.*

could not help saying it was the *loosest* family I ever saw!" Towards the end of the century glazed pottery, some of it in the fashionable willow pattern style, began to be used for W.C. bowls.

In the 1780s W.C.s fitted with valves became available for the first time since Sir John Harrington's invention. A watchmaker, Alexander Cummings, took out a patent in 1775, but the valve was unreliable. Joseph Bramah, a cabinet-maker, patented a greatly improved model in1778 and produced 6000 in his first year, and his company went on making them until 1890 to the same pattern.

In the nineteenth century sanitary arrangements gradually improved on a large scale. As early as 1813, the Earl of Moira's Doddington Park in Leicestershire had two bathrooms and six internal W.C.s.

Very grand fringing *used as both the pelmet and the edging on these elegant Austrian blinds or pull-up curtains makes for a doubly distinguished effect against the quiet richness of the background. Note the elaborate cornice edged in a neat stripe of nutmeg brown to match the picked-out panelling below the window. The old shutters have been left plain to give full rein to the other more lavish ingredients, although many people paint the panels or pick them out in Modigliani-like fashion, and omit any fabric treatment.*

Lady Moira's bathroom had a gilded washstand, a dressing stand with gilded basin, a rosewood book stand and a copper tea kettle for soothing liquid refreshment. Washstands began to be available to the general public, and shaving tables were built with integral mirrors, basins and bidets. Decorated china basins and jugs or pitchers for washing were commonplace.

Hepplewhite designed some elegant little marquetry cases for chamber pots, and, as I have mentioned elsewhere, dining room sideboards often contained a pot cupboard at one end. Sometimes too, shelves containing chamber pots were concealed behind window shutters for the convenience of gentlemen who stayed on drinking after dinner. The cloakroom, or powder room, was yet to be invented.

An original Victorian bathroom *with its old bath, drainage system and floor tiles has been gently titivated with a cleverly placed border which virtually panels the room above the deep dado. It harmonizes but does not coordinate with the curtain borders. The length of the bath more than makes up for any more modern creature comforts, but note the early heated towel rail suspended high on the wall.*

The flower-strewn chintz *is repeated in the windowsill of this bathroom with its deep corner window and leaded panes. The simple arrangement of blue and white china looks particularly good against this setting, and the effect is quintessentially cottage-like with the beams, the short curtains with their casual bows and the soft pale green of the view outside.*

The bathrooms of Victoria and Albert

Even when running water became ubiquitous and its regular use accepted, it was seldom piped above the basement. Thus servants still had to run up and down stairs with jugs of water, and baths and basins remained portable affairs in a great many ingenious shapes: slipper baths, sponge baths, lounge or full baths, sitting or sitz baths, hip baths, fountain baths and travelling baths. Interestingly, Queen Victoria had no bathroom at Buckingham Palace when she came to the throne; and she actually broke up George IV's great six-foot deep bath at the Royal Pavilion in Brighton (it measured 16 by 10 feet and was piped with sea water) to make marble mantelpieces for the palace. Later she did install one bathroom at each of her residences. Prince Albert attempted to replace the old-fashioned commodes inherited from his wife's forbears with new (though not so very new) water closets and drains, after the discovery of 53 overflowing cesspools at Windsor Castle, but his work was cut short by his death and was not resumed until the reign of Edward VII.

A children's bathroom in a nineteenth-century house has been moved well into the twentieth century with its striking colouring: red and white tiles and deep blue floor and walls. There is certainly no need for any other adornment at the window, especially given its painted frame.

Nevertheless, Queen Victoria's bathroom at Osborne on the Isle of Wight is a charming room with all the ingredients now associated with the most covetable of English country house bathrooms. It has a fireplace and overmantel complete with clock and mirror surrounded by portraits, paintings, early family photographs and other memorabilia. A mahogany dressing table stands before the long chintz curtains of the window, and the mahogany-sided marble bath in an alcove has double doors to close it off.

Respectability demands a bathroom

The Queen's subjects were a little more generous with their facilities. By the 1880s, bathrooms were familiar although far from common, and taps with hot and cold water were still rare. Large country houses turned spare bedrooms into bathrooms, which in grand houses might be panelled or hung with tapestries. Such bedrooms might be furnished with flat shallow hip baths, usually painted and grained dark brown outside and cream inside. These were filled from large metal

Red William Morris wallpaper *and a blue and white tiled splashback are an effective combination and make a good background for the nice country house mix of idiosyncratic pictures and objects. A glass painting with an unusual photomontage and a poem is hung below and slightly to the side of a Gothic mirror, where it can be carefully perused from the bath, which is otherwise flanked by a miscellany of interesting prints.*

cans of polished brass or copper, or else painted to match the bath.

There would also be ample washstands with marble tops, splash backs, basins, ewers, soap dishes, brush stands and decorated chamber pots. R.S. Surtees in *Mr Sponge's Sporting Tour* (1853) described a bedroom furnished with "every imaginable luxury", including "hip baths and foot baths, a shower bath, or hot and cold baths adjoining and mirrors innumerable". When water was laid on, plumbing troubles were legendary. *Punch* cartoons featured anguished people enveloped in clouds of steam trying to turn taps on or off.

Still by the end of the nineteenth century almost every respectable house had at least one bathroom converted from a bedroom, and new houses were being built with integral bathrooms with extravagant floor space. Water closets were splendidly handsome affairs for the most part, sculpted and decorated with floral motifs, acanthus leaves, Greek key designs, what you will. In rural areas, however, farmhouses and cottages still had outhouses or privies, close-stools or commodes, and chamber pots remained very much a part of life in bedrooms.

A spacious bath-dressing room *contains many nineteenth-century attributes as well as nods to current times, and is all the more interesting for it. The bath and basin, though edged with mahogany, are definitely by-products of the twentieth century, as are the bidet and the wallpaper. The handsome heavy curtains are of indeterminate age and elegantly drawn back, while the large wardrobe, chest, medal display case, pitcher and ewer, mirror, clock and leather chair with swan-ended arms are all from a previous era.*

The fall of the bathroom

Specially built bathrooms often had windows of stained glass with heavily tasselled curtains. Some had patterned wallpaper, but tiles soon became popular for walls and floors. Baths were elaborately decorated on the outside and many had marble veining inside. As the twentieth century wore on, the bathroom became less and less a furnished room, shrinking gradually to become a practical tiled shell with its fittings and plumbing on one wall.

The contemporary country bathroom

Today, a country style bathroom is once again more of a room, or it is at least more comfortably decorated. There will, if possible, be a good wide ledge around the bath to hold toiletries and pretty glass and china. Bath and basin sides might be panelled in mahogany, or painted, or papered, or tiled. Walls will be wallpapered (and glazed for practicality), or painted decoratively, and they will certainly be hung with every sort of memorabilia. If there is a good-sized window, it will

A lesser splash *Another modern detail from the all but nineteenth-century bathroom pictured opposite. The bath is centrally placed, which can be an ideal position if the bathroom is of a generous size.*

be curtained, or shaded, or both. There will be plants, and pretty tiles, and very probably a carpet. The greatest luxury, of course, would be a working fireplace, for the old practice of taking a hot bath in front of the bedroom fire lingers on as an ideal.

Country house cloakrooms, or powder rooms, are again a turn-of-the century convenience, an essential to a country house and a great improvement on the old dining room arrangements. Contemporary English country house cloakrooms will almost certainly be hung with photographs, press cuttings, postcards, prints, any sort of memorabilia or whimsy that takes the owner's fancy. The romantic version has them with mahogany panelling, converted etched glass Edwardian oil lamps, generous mirrors and an air of opulent comfort left over from the Edwardian era, a far cry from the cold, damp, unwelcoming space that was the British country cloakroom from the 1920s to the 1960s. But along with every other room in the house, the best of British cloakrooms are a comfortable amalgam of the components and traditions of the past, backed, at last, with adequate plumbing.

CHAPTER NINE

ENGLISH COUNTRY STYLE IN PRACTICE

It must be apparent to anyone reading this book that at the moment there is very little that is innovative in decoration. From the seventeenth century on, people were marbling, distressing, graining, staining, lacquering, using all kinds of wall coverings, inventing new window treatments and bed treatments, trying out new ideas for floors, and making all sorts of experiments with furniture finishes. Much the same rush and coia matting as we use today has been in and out of fashion since medieval times. Magnificent carpets and rugs have been produced for centuries. The only real advances have been in upholstery, convenience and lighting.

Nevertheless, it is useful to know how certain effects connected with English country decoration are achieved, and how to make short cuts that approximate to the real thing for half the expense.

I have divided this chapter into sections on wall treatments using paint and using fabric, floor treatments, and window and bed treatments, with a brief guide to furniture renovation principles. Readers who see in any of the rooms previously illustrated a design or finish that they particularly like can refer to the relevant section for advice. I have also shown a number of sketched suggestions for windows and beds that have been used in various houses over the centuries, but not all of which appear in the photographs.

WALL TREATMENTS: PAINT

Most periods used distinctive colours. Many owners of old houses, or, if not old, of houses that they wish to appear mellow, use a synthesis of colours from the centuries – a suggestion or interpretation rather than a simulation. It is useful therefore to have a feel, both for the colours appropriate to a particular period, and for the play of light and the effects of shade and fading. The latter is garnered most easily by studying paintings; those of the Impressionists are particularly helpful for this.

For example, the effect of the Palladian influence was to introduce Italian pinks, terracottas and a sort of apricot-terracotta. The late Georgians used French greys, pinks, pale blues, buffs, light yellows, lilacs and greens. Adam used intense colours, employing, for example, a pink that is much stronger than most people would think of using today, even in this society used to colour; and at the end of the eighteenth century colours began to get heavier and in came darker blues, yellows and apricots, apple greens, jades, reds and browns. Colours were also influenced by the backgrounds of Chinese and Indian fabrics.

There was, of course, nothing like the range of commercial paint colours available now, so colours had to be mixed as a painter mixes tones on his palette. Moreover, the inferior grinding of pigments often gave an uneven quality, a sort of textured effect. According to John Cornforth in his *The Inspiration of the Past*, the late John Fowler, that master of the painting of rooms, always preferred water paints to modern emulsion or latex paints. This was because they gave the worn effect of old colour if applied in thin glazes, and Fowler often insisted on the translucent over-painting of white to give the right sort of old texture. The important thing, he thought, was always to show a bit of undercoat through a top coat; and always to break the colour and texture of any dark colour to prevent it from looking too solid.

To get a non-commercial mixture of colours to seem right in a room, it is essential to be patient and to try different samples in different lights. I always recommend people first of all to try out different techniques (ragging, dragging, stippling, etc.) on large pieces of primed board, and then to test different samples in different lights on the walls in question. Interestingly, nearly all John Fowler's colours were taken from pieces of fabric rather than from paint samples, and in order to emulate the liveliness of, say, silk, or a weave, a paint surface simply has to be broken.

A particular skill is to use paint to emphasize the framework of a room – the cornice, mouldings, dado rail, skirting or baseboards, and to relate the chimneypiece to the doorcase. In simple rooms, without such architectural details, it is quite possible to suggest them by, for example, lining out the walls to suggest panelling, painting *trompe l'oeil* mouldings, applying strips of mouldings of varying size, or adding trims below the cornice – or ceiling if there is no cornice – down the corners and along the tops of skirting or baseboards, just as they did so often in preceding centuries. Again, much effect can be gained by varying texture as well

as tone: by, for example, dragging a dado and skirting or baseboards and ragging any reliefs, leaving the recesses smooth. Dados can be suggested, incidentally, by running lengths of moulding around the room at chair-top height.

Glazes

A glaze is a transparent film, usually tinted, applied to an opaque base. It is used in most decorative finishes – dragging, stippling and ragging – and adds richness and depth to any wall treatment. If a glaze is a hue in the family of the base coat, the resulting colour will be a delicately modified and deepened tone within the same family. On the other hand, if the glaze and the base coat are in different colour groups, the resulting colour will be an entirely new one, with the additional richness of translucence. Any glazing technique will look best with colours that are similar in intensity, or with a darker colour over a lighter one. A Sienna brown glaze over a deep green base, for example, will produce a lovely terracotta; dark grey over Pompeian red will look like Moroccan leather; dark green over a medium green will turn walls to jade.

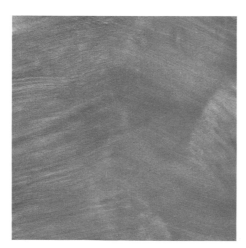

Glazing

Glazing liquids are available at good paint stores and come in half pints, quarts and gallons. A half pint will cover about 60 square feet, a quart about 250 square feet, and a gallon approximately 1000 square feet.

Generally you will need less glaze than paint because you will be applying a much thinner coat. It looks thick to begin with, rather like canned cream of chicken soup. If it seems too thick, it can be thinned gently with mineral spirits or paint thinner.

When you come to tint the glaze, you should start out with a small amount of tinting medium and then build up the amount of colour until you get the shade you want. Squeeze a blob of artist's oil paint, or stainer, into an old saucepan and stir in several tablespoons of turpentine or mineral spirits; mix thoroughly until smooth. Add about one cup of unthinned glaze to the pan and mix thoroughly. Test this mixture on a small area of wall prepared with your base coat. If you want to add more colour, or to change the colour slightly, mix a bit more tint with some turpentine in another old pan or disposable aluminium pie tin. Add this to the glaze and test again. Continue until you get the exact shade you want, but never add the tinting colour, stainer, or artist's oil colour straight from the tube as it will not homogenize readily.

Be sure your base coat is completely dry before applying the glaze, and apply it evenly and confidently, keeping the glaze at the right consistency and working quickly to avoid drips and clumps. Once the glaze is up on the wall it will dry quite fast.

When you have glazed your walls and the finish has dried for 24 hours, you may want to give them a coat of polyurethane varnish. This will not only add protection but will also tend to darken the finish slightly, giving it a nice mellow antiquated look. How much it will darken depends on how clear the polyurethane is, and how many coats you apply. The polyurethane comes from a paint shop in flat, semi-gloss and high gloss finishes. Apply with a roller and brush it out with a large brush or cheap foam pad to get rid of any bubbles. Whatever happens, do not apply any subsequent coats until the first has been dry for at least 24 hours, even if it does feel dry to the touch before then.

Dragging

Dragging is achieved by applying a glaze of transparent colour over a chosen undercoat,

Dragging

and then "dragging" the glaze – or brushing it down – with a wide, dry brush. The glaze is normally a darker hue than the undercoat, and the resulting softly textured look of fine, irregular vertical striations gives a rich, distinguished effect.

Professional painters use expensive brushes called "floggers", especially designed for dragging, but for most amateurs a standard five-inch paint brush will work well as long as you work quickly, since each "drag" will cover less area. You can also use a graining tool, which is like a three-inch wooden triangle with either a fine, medium or coarse tooth comb. Another option is a window washer's rubber squeegee with teeth cut into it, but this will give much bigger striations than the subtle brush work. Since the glaze dries quickly, you will almost certainly need two people on the job, one to lay on the glaze, the other to follow along and do the "drags".

Stippling

Stippling is a little less difficult than dragging, but it is just as decorative. It is often used in conjunction with dragging, for example, dragged mouldings and stippled ground in door panels, or on panelled walls or on skirting or baseboards. It can look as soft as chamois, or as pitted as an orange skin, for stippled walls are dappled with flecks of colour without emphatic definition, allowing the base colour to become part of the whole.

Stippling

As with dragging, the tinted glaze is applied to the chosen undercoat and then removed with a professional stippling brush or a shoe or scrubbing brush. You can also use a roller or a large sponge to get a more muted look.

Ragging

Ragging is a rather freer and more raggedy version of stippling. It is much more free-flowing and irregular, and therefore easier to do alone. It is also good in a limited space because the somewhat "cloudy" effect creates an illusion of airiness and softness. Unlike the dry brushes or tools used for dragging and stippling, ragging is done with a bunched-up rag, wetted in turpentine or mineral spirits before use. The coarser the rag – anything can be used from cheese cloth to hessian – the crisper the texture. Try rolling pastels over a creamy white ground, or, for an extremely subtle look, use a tinted white over white, or an umber-tinted cream over cream. Again, a mixture of ragging, dragging, stippling and plain paint brings out mouldings and architecture very well.

Ragging

Lacquering

Lacquering is an ancient craft, which originated in the Far East. The process is extremely time-consuming if it is done properly, since it needs up to 40 coats of lacquer, each buffed and burnished before the next coat can be applied, but the effect is rich and deep and extremely hard-wearing. True

lacquer, derived from the oriental lac tree, is a kind of varnish, usually containing pigment, that dries to a hard surface. It is difficult to obtain and very expensive. Happily, there are a number of facsimile techniques which are a great deal cheaper and less time-consuming, although they still require a good deal of patience.

If you are lacquering whole walls (as opposed to a piece of furniture), you will need to start with absolutely smooth surfaces. The simplest method is to apply a couple of coats of clear, thinned-down eggshell or high gloss polyurethane varnish over two or three coats of oil-based flat or eggshell paint, depending on how shiny you want the surface.

A more complex method is to apply a series of tinted glazes over a base coat. The whole is then polyurethaned for protection and increased depth. This creates a remarkably pretty pearled effect. Do remember that when applying any sort of lacquer to any sort of surface, you must ensure that your room is totally free from dust.

Stencilling

Another old craft is stencilling, which is based on the repetition of a single, simple design. This is good for ceilings, floors and furniture as well as walls and, using fabric paint, for plain cotton, linen and sheets. It is a decorative solution that can be as pretty or as idiosyncratic as you like for a fraction of the cost of wallpaper and other wallcoverings. It also looks good superimposed on the various decorative finishes already described. There are a variety of ready-made stencils but it is amusing to try your own. Designs can be culled from anywhere: a motif from wallpaper or fabric (which can be traced), from a carpet border, an old quilt, a magazine, a book, or even the pattern on a moulding.

Keep the design as simple as possible and consider its size: you will probably want to make it bigger or smaller. If you are unable to do this accurately freehand, take the design to a printing shop and have it blown up or reduced to the scale that you want. Then trace the design on to tracing paper, isolating the various parts to be cut out. If, for example, you use a flower motif, you will need to isolate the petals, the centre, the stem and the

leaves. There should be a gap between each of the parts, so outline them so that they fit together but do not touch. The next step is to colour the parts, using crayons. Take several tracings so that you can experiment with the colouring until you are satisfied.

Work out the distance that you want your design to be from the ceiling or the skirting or baseboards, or furniture or fabric edge, and buy a piece of acetate – available from art supply stores – large enough to cover your design plus this distance. You will then be able to butt the edge of the acetate against the ceiling, baseboards, etc. and use it as your guide.

Place the acetate over your design, leaving the space that you want between the design and the edge of the acetate, and secure it firmly with masking tape. Trace the design on to the acetate and then cut out the pattern, using an X-Acto knife, or similar, fitted with either No 16 or No 11 blades. To keep a smooth edge, don't lift the point of the blade, but turn the design as you cut. When you have finished cutting, the stencil is ready.

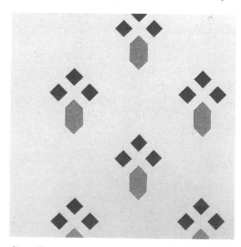

Stencilling

The best paints to use are artists' acrylic colours, in tubes. Since these acrylics come only in concentrated colours, you will need to mix them beforehand in paper cups or on paper plates if you want faded or muted tones. But do not thin the paint because it may then run out below the stencil's edges.

Secure the acetate to the surface to be stencilled with masking tape but first stick the tape on your forearm a few times to remove the excess stickiness and prevent paint, varnish or material fibres being pulled off with the tape when you release the acetate.

Take a small piece of sponge – it is best to cut up a whole sponge – and dip it into one of the colours. Remove the excess paint by pouncing it – vigorously dabbing the sponge up and down – on a clean portion of a plate. Dab the paint on to the surface through the relevant opening in the stencil. With experience you will find the different effects that can be obtained with a very light up and down movement. Do one colour at a time. When you have filled in all the cut-out areas, untape the acetate and carefully lift it straight from the surface. Use a small artist's brush to touch up any small errors and to add any finishing touches. It is also a good idea to use the brush for tricky, thin areas like flower stems. Now repeat the design in the next area.

If you suffer a crisis of confidence about transferring the colours to the relevant surface, there is a "cheater's" method for beginners, suggested by Vera Crozer, a superb stenciller in Connecticut, USA. Instead of painting through the stencil with pieces of sponge, take a No 3 pencil and lightly draw the outlines of all the cut-out areas. Remove the stencil and then paint directly on to the surface with small brushes, referring to your original tracing to make sure that you are keeping track of which colours go where.

Once the stencilling is completely dry, give the surface (except for fabrics) a final coat of polyurethane to preserve the stencilling and make the surface washable.

Conservatory Wallpaper

This method of painting paper, originally conceived for a conservatory, is both very effective and economical. Begin by making a wood frame about 2ft by 2ft and fix a piece of plastic in the bottom to make a large tray; it has to be able to hold water so use plastic sheeting up the sides if necessary. Fill the tray with water and then spatter the surface with artists' oil paints in the colours to suit your room. Green is the obvious choice but

the result is more effective if you use more than one colour, for example, two shades of green and a greeny-blue. Spatter the paint by knocking the loaded paint brush against your hand, and cover most but not all of the surface.

Cut some heavy-duty lining paper to the required length and get a helper to hold one end while you hold the other. Lightly drop the paper on to the surface of the water, dabbing at it in places where the paint is not sticking – usually the edges. Lift the paper away from the tray quickly and put it to dry against a wall or on the floor or a place where paint drops do not matter.

WALL TREATMENTS: FABRICS

For centuries wall hangings were common in country houses. Old paintings show not just tapestries, which sometimes completely cover a wall, but also wall fabrics with elaborately fringed and tasselled cappings. In the seventeenth and eighteenth centuries fabric was often battened on to the walls over an upholstered lining and the nail marks covered in thin fillets of gold leather, or braid or trim of some sort might go under the cornice, and run around the top of the dado, down the corners and around doors.

Regency stripe fabric

Fabric coverings can look marvellous and are excellent insulation for draughty country plaster as well as a good disguise for less than perfect surfaces. It is, however, expensive to

have a professional decorator to fabric your walls. One less expensive solution is to run thin brass rods or dowels all round the top of the walls just below the ceiling or cornice and to hang hemmed lengths of fabric from them, like draperies or curtains, looping the material back over doors, windows and fireplaces. This can look very effective in bedrooms, and paintings, mirrors and prints can be hung on top of the fabric.

Another way of disguising crumbly plaster or sheet rock is to shirr walls with a lightweight fabric such as tight-weave muslin, cheesecloth or sheeting. Again, mount rods or dowels just below the ceiling, but this time also fix them just above the skirting or base boards, and above any doors, and above and below any windows. You will need to allow for fabric about three times the wall's width, because the effect must not seem skimped. Hem the fabric at both ends to accommodate the rods or dowels and gather it along the rod so that it shirrs naturally.

Shirring

If you want the walls to be tight-covered and do not want to call in a specialist, you can achieve a near-professional effect with the use of a staplegun. It is best to choose a close-weave fabric, such as tightly woven cotton, velvet, corduroy, denim, flannel, broadcloth, linen with a touch of polyester or two-ply chambray. You then staple the top and bottom of each length of fabric to the wall at about three-inch intervals. The fabric

has to be "seamed", which looks more professional if the lengths are sewn together. However, if you want a panelled effect, you can simply overlap each fabric length and staple down the join. The staple marks can then be covered with some sort of trim: braid, grosgrain ribbon, velvet ribbon, painted fillets of wood, or even lengths of picture frame moulding in natural wood, or gilded or silvered. Gluing, however, often causes the joins to harden, and there is another, rather less simple way to join the fabric which is almost indistinguishable from sewing.

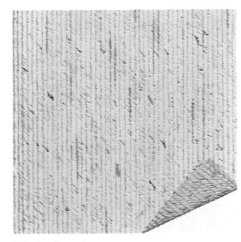

Wool wallcovering

Staple the top, bottom and edge of the first fabric length to the wall, then lay a line of small beads of glue down the fabric about half an inch in from the edge. Line up your next panel, with the "good" side facing the wall, so that it covers the first stapled and glued panel, press the fabric into the glue and staple it in place just beyond the glue line. Fold back the newly attached panel and continue stapling as you did for the first panel. Always begin stapling the panels at the top, smoothing, not stretching, the fabric as you go, and finish by stapling the bottom, giving the fabric a little tug to make it taut.

An almost foolproof system of attaching fabric to walls is provided by Fabritrack, which is available in both Britain and North America. It consists of long plastic strips with

Suede wallcovering

"jaws" to hide ragged edges, and an adhesive strip to hold the fabric tight. The strips are attached just below the ceiling or moulding and just above the skirting or baseboards.

If you want an upholstered look, you will have to batten the fabric, i.e. stretch panels of fabric between battens – laths or thin strips of wood – fixed horizontally along the top and bottom of the wall, in the same way as the Fabritrack. Vertical strips of wood are then added at six-feet intervals and the fabric is seamed where necessary to join the lengths. Before fixing the fabric, you line the space between the battens with "bump", a special padding material for walls, or with some sort of Acrilan padding, which you can staple to the battens. The first fabric panel is then attached by centring it between the outside edge of the first vertical lath and the middle of the next one, with the top of the fabric level with the top of the horizontal batten. Tack it lightly in position, starting at the top in the middle and stretching the fabric to either side. Then staple it and remove the tacks. To neaten the joins between the fabric panels, use strips of cardboard the same size as the battens. Place the second panel, "good" side down, over the first panel so that their cut edges align. Lay a cardboard strip over the join and staple through card and fabric on to the batten. Fold the second panel back. Continue in this way. As before, any staple marks can be covered with trim.

205

FLOOR TREATMENTS

Many old houses have wood floors that can be renovated to their original handsome state. Provided that they do not have many gaps and splintered ends, they can be sanded down, stained if necessary, then sealed and polished. If they are in bad condition, the gaps can be filled and the boards painted,

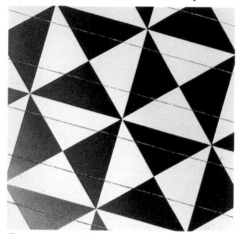

Pattern-painted floor

either with deck paint or, better, with ordinary gloss paint that is given a finishing coat of clear varnish. In fact, if you use polyurethane, you can use almost any type of paint underneath. The trick is to apply several coats of polyurethane, letting each coat dry

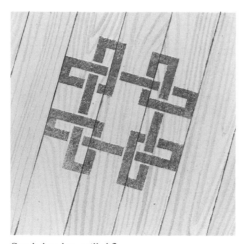

Sanded and stencilled floor

for 24 hours before applying the next. Painted floors can stand up to a surprising amount of wear and tear if you give them a new coat of polyurethane each year. Traditional country colours are dark grey-blue or deep terracotta, or you might try a sparkling white or cream. Such painted floors – before they have been varnished – make an excellent base for stencils, perhaps using an overall carpet-like design, or a border motif. Stencilling methods are the same as those given for walls. Or you might put down floorcloths.

Floorcloths

Painted floorcloths, made of canvas, were as popular in England during the eighteenth and early nineteenth centuries as they were in America and only went out of use when linoleum came in. Most designs – and floorcloths lend themselves to a great variety – work out best if you first draw the design on graph paper and then transfer it to a grid drawn on the canvas. You can use readymade stencils or make up your own design, perhaps taking a motif from a fabric in the room, or from an oriental rug pattern or old quilt. If ideas are short, or artistic talent is lacking, a floorcloth will still look good in a plain colour with a contrasting border. It will also look better in darker colours, since most cloths crack with time and pastels show the cracks more obviously.

You will need unprimed or, more expensive, primed canvas, available from artists' supply stores, which includes an allowance for a 1½in edging; cheap white water-base paint for priming if you have bought unprimed canvas; water or latex or emulsion paint for the main or background colour; a large paintbrush and cheap sponge brushes in a variety of sizes; a small paintbrush and tubes of acrylic artists' paints in the colours that you need; a pencil, ruler, masking tape, polyurethane and white glue.

If the canvas was bought unprimed, it may need two coats of white water-based paint for good coverage. Allow it to dry thoroughly. Lay the primed canvas on a clean floor and cut it so that it is 1½in wider all round than your design. Pencil a line round the canvas, 1½in from the edge, to mark where the canvas will later be turned under. Cover the

Painted floorcloth

canvas with a coat of paint of the main background colour, painting right up to the pencil line. For a very neat edge, stick masking tape along the line, but this is rarely necessary. The colour and quality of the paint may mean that you need to use two or three coats of paint, allowing each coat to dry before applying the next. When the background paint is completely dry, lightly chalk in your grid – if you are using one – and then the outline of the design.

Mix your acrylic paint and begin painting or stencilling, starting with the strongest colours first and making sure that you mix enough paint for each area; matching a second mix can be hard. Allow the paint to dry thoroughly, and then give the canvas two or three coats of polyurethane, either flat or semi-gloss. When the final coat is quite dry, turn the canvas over and carefully fold under the borders. Snip off a triangular piece of canvas from each corner, which will allow the folded-under canvas to lie flat. Lay a heavy bead of glue in the fold, then brush out the glue to the edges, and repeat along the fold. Press the border down and hold it in place with weights until the glue is completely dry.

If the paint has cracked slightly when the floorcloth is turned over, touch up the edges. Lay the floorcloth on a smooth hard-surfaced

floor and do not put a pad underneath or it will crack when it is walked on. A light coat of liquid wax, and perhaps also a light new coat of polyurethane every year, will preserve it well.

Faux Tiling

Another solution to improve an old floor in bad condition is to "tile" it with squares of stencilled or painted masonite or wood fibre. The "tiles" can also be "marbled", or painted like stone, or given any other decorative finish, and they can be laid in any design wished; a candidate might be the handsome stone and marble floor shown on p. 108, which could also be emulated in linoleum or vinyl. You can ask your local lumberyard or timber merchants to cut the wood into squares of the size that you want. Prime, paint, stencil and varnish the tiles before gluing or nailing them down; dampen the backs first to prevent them curling at the edges. This sort of floor needs to be given the same coats of flat or semi-gloss polyurethane as any other painted finish.

Faux tiling

Marbling

It helps to have a real piece of marble or at least a photograph, to copy, and to use the more common colours – beige, off-white, grey, grey-green. Begin by priming the "tiles" with a coat of white latex or emulsion paint, then follow it with a coat of flat or eggshell

Marbled faux tiles

oil-based paint in white or off-white, or the base colour of any other marble you might like. When this is dry, sand the tiles lightly with fine sandpaper and then rub them with a light coat of three parts white or mineral spirit mixed with one part linseed oil and a drop of liquid dryers, available from good paint stores.

Next brush on a glaze (see Glazing), tinted a slightly darker colour than your base coat, in an irregular pattern, with some patches in broad raggedy bands or drifts. Before the glaze dries completely, dab the entire surface with a rag or sponge dipped in turpentine or white or mineral spirits. This will soften the edge of the glaze and, by removing some of the glaze here and there, will produce the right mottled effect.

Using a small brush or feather, and two stronger tones of glaze or very thinned-down oil-based paint in the colours of the marble you envisage, run narrow veins across the cloudy background. These may run in the same general direction as the broader, cloudy background drifts or in the opposite direction, or in both directions, depending on your taste. Thinned-down oil paint may be easier to use than glaze since it dries more slowly.

When your veining seems right, dab at the surface with a turpentine-dampened rag or sponge to blur the glaze again somewhat. If the marbling still looks too harsh or well-

defined, drag a wide paint brush – either dry or dampened with turpentine – across the whole thing. Finally, again using a small brush or feather and the strong colours that you used for the veining, mark in very subtly a few short contrasting veins here and there, alongside and/or over the now smudgy veins. When all the "tiles" are finished and thoroughly dry, fix them in place and give the whole floor a few coats of semi-gloss polyurethane.

Stone Effects

A look of stone can be achieved in a similar way to marbling. Prepare the "tiles" by covering them roughly with a coat of white oil-based paint mixed with two parts of white or mineral spirit. Then apply a similar mix of paint, tinted with grey artists' oil paint or a stainer, to the parts missed by the first coat. Rub over the still wet colours with a sponge to mix them roughly together, then flick on white or mineral spirits with a clean brush knocked against a piece of wood, so that small holes appear and spread a little to look like stone. When dry, fix the tiles to the floor and varnish as usual with several coats of semi-gloss polyurethane, allowing 24 hours between each coat.

Sandstone faux tiles

Staining

Floors can be made to look much richer by staining them, which clarifies and highlights

the original grain. Stains are available in oil-, water- and alcohol-based mediums, each of which gives a slightly different finish and is applied in a different way. Pigmented oil stains generally give the most lustrous finish; they are mixed with turpentine or mineral spirits and dry relatively slowly. Water-based stains are easily applied and soak into the wood quickly, but they tend to dry rather splotchily. Alcohol-based stains dry almost instantly and can be tricky for the amateur to use since it is easy to re-cover a dry section by accident, which builds up the colour and gives an uneven look. Oil stains may well be preferable because they seep into the wood so slowly that there is time to adjust the depth of tone. Any excess must, however, be wiped off or it will harden into a gummy mess. Water- or alcohol-based stains leave very little excess to remove.

The more coats of stain that you apply, the deeper the tone will be, and the final protective coats will darken the colour even more. Also, any given stain will have a different effect on different types of wood, so try it out first on an out-of-the-way spot.

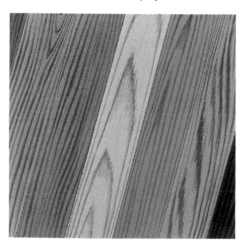

Wood-stained boards

You can achieve very close approximations of some of the marvellous early parquetry patterns by using two or three different colour wood stains. It is time-consuming but worth it. You might alternate two or three shades on individual boards of a standard or parquet floor, or use two or three geometric shapes and two or more different shades of stain to make your own parquetry patterns on a standard strip floor. Work out the design on graph paper and then transfer it to a chalked-out grid on the floor. You will need to score the floor lightly to outline the shapes, so that the stain does not spread to adjacent areas. Staining of this sort will also look very distinguished as a border. In the nineteenth century, farm bedrooms often had alternately stained boards as a border around a carpet or large rug, and a plain wood floor can look extremely handsome with a geometric border.

If the wood floor is in bad condition, large Masonite, fibrewood or plyboard squares, as described in "Faux Tiling", could be stained and fixed to the floor to achieve an impressive new look in, say, a large hall or dining room. Or squares can be marked out on an existing strip floor, keeping half of them natural and half stained white.

Bleaching

Bleaching means removing some of the natural colour of the wood to achieve a clean, light, airy effect, especially suitable for a mid to late eighteenth-century look. Ordinary household bleach usually gives the desired result: scrub it in well, let it work for ten to fifteen minutes, then rinse it off with water. If the result is not light enough, repeat the

Bleached boards

process until the desired effect is achieved. No matter how well you rinse, some bleach will remain and the surface will need to be neutralized, which you can do with a solution of one part vinegar to one part water. Rinse the floor one final time with clear water and allow to dry completely. All this bleaching and rinsing will have raised the grain of the wood, so the floor should now be lightly sanded, then vacuumed and wiped clean before applying at least two coats of poly-urethane, waiting, as usual, 24 hours for each coat to dry.

Lightening

Lightening floors is done simply by painting the floor white, off-white or cream, then wiping off most of the paint, letting it dry and polyurethaning. Work with about nine feet of floor at a time. Brush on oil-based paint – stark white can be given a subtle tone by adding a dash of artists' oil paint in an earthy colour. After a few minutes, wipe off most of the paint with a clean dry rag, working against the grain. The idea is to leave a slight film of paint over the entire surface, with small crooks and crevices in the wood filled with thicker dabs and slivers of paint, to give an overall "antiqued" look. It is especially effective on soft woods like pine. Allow the floor to dry overnight, then polyurethane in the usual way.

Flagstones and Tiles

Many old country houses in England, especially in the West country, the Midlands and the North, have flagstone floors in kitchens, halls and passageways. Houses in the southern and eastern counties are more likely to have old quarry tiles, bricks or "pamments", which are nice old terracotta squares – the East Anglian version of French Provençal tiles. If you look around and haunt demolition sites and builders' yards, you can often find old flags, bricks and pamments, or you can make reasonable approximations of at least the flagstones and bricks by thoroughly ill-treating modern concrete slabs and new bricks. Lay the concrete slabs first and then bash them with a hammer or chisel to rough up the edges. Rub them with a mixture of black and brown shoe

Quarry tiles

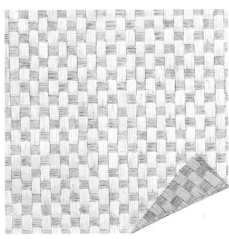

Matting (left and above); light, medium and coarse textures in basic weave, large loops and two-tone herringbone patterns.

polish, wipe it off; rub mud into them, wipe it off; give them numerous coats of wax polish, using an electric polisher to finish off each time. Eventually, with enough ill treatment and enough polishing, they will end up looking pleasantly old. The same sort of treatment can be meted out to bricks, which anyway look good laid in squares or in a herringbone pattern.

Matting

Another country flooring that has been used in the British Isles for hundreds of years is matting. It sets off the humblest or the grandest furniture, or a mixture of both, and looks good topped by rugs of any type. It is also quite cheap.

There are five basic varieties: rush, coia, sisal, seagrass and maize. They range in texture from chunky woven rush – available in the United Kingdom through Waveney Apple Growers – to very fine, pale maize. Coia, which comes from coconuts, and sisal, from the leaves of the agave plant, range in colour from pale honey-gold to darkish brown and are available in a number of different weaves. Try to get them latex- or vinyl-backed for durability and to stop the dirt falling through. Rush, seagrass and maize range from a very pale greenish-cream to mid-brown; they are inclined to get dry and crumble, so they should be moistened occasionally, using a plant spray.

RENOVATING FURNITURE

The restoration of fine antique furniture is a labour of love and a fine art, but other, much cheaper furniture can often be made to look very decorative, and in some cases can be restored to former glory, by giving it a painted finish. For a description of this art, you need to refer to such books as Isabel O'Neil's classic *The Art of the Painted Finish for Furniture and Decoration*, and Jocasta Innes's *Paint Magic*, but it is useful to know how to strip and prepare the surface of furniture ready for such painting, or for refinishing.

Leave plenty of room around the object to be worked on, which ideally should be in a light, airy space where it can stay undisturbed until completion. All hardware should be removed from the piece if possible and put carefully aside. Have on hand a selection of sandpaper of varying coarseness. Sanding blocks, which come in various sizes, from 1½in by 2in upwards, are particularly helpful for fine surfaces: the layer of felt around which the sandpaper is wrapped cushions the stroke to help avoid scratches. Except when using a sheet of sandpaper to wrap around a block, work with a quarter of a sheet at a time. Divide it up by tearing it four

209

ways against a steel edge. If you have narrow mouldings or similar areas to smooth, use fine strips. Carvings can sometimes be abrased with a sharpened typewriter eraser.

A light sanding of the surface is often all that is needed to create a bond for the paint, though a little more pressure may be required to eliminate a deep crack. If, however, you have a piece of furniture that has already been painted over many times, and inexpertly at that, you will first have to resort to a paint remover. Well-painted but faded furniture, on the other hand, will only need to be sanded with 100 garnet paper. It is important to discriminate between the dents and irregularities, the worn patches and cracks of mellow old age and the blemishes that arise from carelessness, such as cigarette burns, scratches and ring marks from glasses and cups. Change the sandpaper when it is full of residue from the old surface, and keep the strokes even, following the direction of the grain unless the design of the piece dictates otherwise, as, for example, in a table with a drawer.

A coarse wood filler can be used to infill large holes, cracks and broken mouldings, though any big cavity should be lined with a resin glue before it is filled, and if an outside edge needs repair a small nail should be driven into the cavity to anchor the filling. When the filler is dried, it should be sanded with 100 garnet paper and then surfaced with fine filler. When this filler is dry, sand it smooth with 220 garnet paper and then shellack it.

Small holes, fine cracks and open seams can be treated with a fine grain or vinyl filler. Take scrapings off the top of the grain filler with a damp palette knife and mix them with water on a plate until a thick paste forms: water should never be added to the can. Vinyl filler can be used directly from the can with a palette knife, orange stick or finger; after a brief wait to allow it to set, wipe away the residue. Sand down with 220 garnet paper and shellack them.

Replacing Missing Carvings
Water putty can be used to duplicate an existing piece of carving so that a missing identical piece can be replaced. Apply oil or petroleum jelly to the existing carving and cover it heavily with coarse filler. This coating forms a negative mould. Allow it to dry, then remove it carefully and grease the cavity before filling it with putty. Leave it to set, then remove the positive mould, allow it to harden, and use a sharp carving tool to point it up. After shellacking, it can be glued in place with a resin glue: smear each of the broken sides, press them together and wipe off any residue with a damp cloth.

Shellacking
White shellac should always be diluted with an equal amount of denatured alcohol and stored away from light in a glass container. Metal causes it to darken. It should never be applied in damp weather or if the surface is damp; the windows should be closed and the room temperature be around 70°F. Keep a brush specially for the process: the best brush is a 1½ or 2in "cutter" or white French bristle brush. Remove excess shellac from the loaded brush by pressing against the inside of the container – if it is drawn across the top, air bubbles are created. Use quick even strokes with no overlap. Once properly shellacked, a piece should be ready for whatever finish has been decided upon.

Period Colours
It helps to achieve the right effect if you know the sort of colours used in a particular period on painted furniture. During the eighteenth century, for example, Hepplewhite furniture usually combined green, black, blue and buff with multicolour decoration. Sheraton and Adam, however, used pastel green, fawn, pink and mauve with white and gold enrichment. The Regency was more restrained, using cream, grey or black with gold decoration or a dark bronzed green. The Victorians were much more eclectic and used designs in all sorts of colours, though often on cream and green backgrounds.

WINDOW AND BED TREATMENTS
Window and bed treatments were often paired in the past and the line illustrations here show some of the more usual designs of the eighteenth and nineteenth centuries.

curtain is used for any kind of fabric hanging, whereas in America curtain is most often used for "stationary" window coverings or what the English call dress curtains, i.e. curtains that are purely for decoration or softening effects and cannot be pulled across. "Draperies", on the other hand, is generally the American term for fabric window coverings that pull.

Window Terms

The following is a brief alphabetical guide to commonly used window terms:

Austrian shade: A gently ruched shade or blind, which is also known in Britain as a festoon blind. It has rows of vertical shirring and can be raised and lowered by cords threaded through rings, which are attached to the back of the shade at regular intervals.

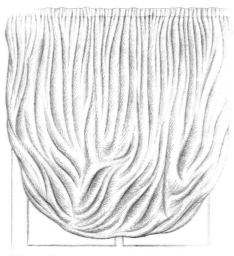

Balloon curtain

Blind: English term for shade. Also used in the US for shades made of matchstick, bamboo, etc.

Café curtain: A short curtain hung from a rod and going half way across a window, as in French cafés. This sort of curtaining is sometimes hung in a double tier and is a useful treatment for windows that open inwards or face directly on to a street, since the tier system gives both light and privacy.

Bed treatments

(Left) *Four-poster with traditional full drapes (top); back drape falling from wall-fixed coronet (centre); four-poster with canopy and back and partial side drapes (below).*

(Above) *Half-tester with back drapes (top); canopied four-poster with open sides (below).*

Many people get their curtains and draperies made by professionals, but it is useful to understand the somewhat complicated vocabulary involved. Window terminology varies widely between the US and Europe. In England, for example, the word

Austrian or festoon curtain

Backing: The special material laminated to roller shade fabric to act as a lining, a stiffener, and a blocker of unwelcome daylight in the early mornings.

Balloon shade: A shade or blind with deep inverted pleats which create a billowing balloon-like effect. Like an Austrian blind, it is pulled up and down by cords threaded through rings attached to the back.

Café curtain with scalloped edge

Casement window: A window that opens on vertical hinges.

Cornice: A wooden frame or pelmet mounted

211

over a window treatment to hide the hardware (or strip lights). It can be painted, stained or covered with matching or contrasting fabric, and may be straight or shaped.

Curtain: In the US, a stationary window covering, or headed length of fabric attached to a rod or track and used to soften a window frame; in Europe, wider widths of similarly headed fabric which can be pulled backwards and forwards across a window.

Drapes: Headed window coverings which can be pulled across a window. They are suspended either from a track or from a pole of some sort.

Festoon blind: See Austrian shade.

Finial: The decorative ends of a curtain rod, usually made of wood or brass.

Heading: The top of curtains or drapes, which might be in the form of gathers, pencil

Pencil pleat heading

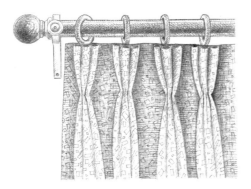

Pinch pleat heading

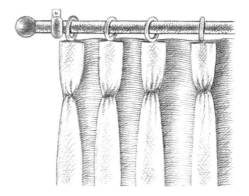

Goblet pleat heading

pleats, pinch pleats, box pleats, scallops, smocking, shirring, etc.

Hourglass curtain: A curtain stretched between two rods, fixed at the top and bottom of the window, and tied in the middle to show a triangle of window pane at either side.

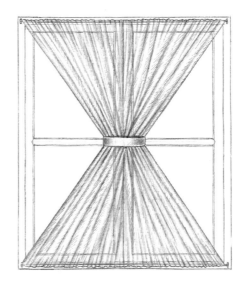

Hourglass curtain

Lace Curtain: As it says; much used in Edwardian country houses.

Leading edge: The inner edge of a curtain, drape or blind, which is often bound or bordered. (Hence: "we'll border the leading edges".)

Mullions: The narrow wood members that separate panes of glass.

Muslin curtain: Like lace, much used in the nineteenth and early twentieth century.

Pattern repeat: A design term for one or more motifs repeated either vertically or horizontally on a fabric. Mention the repeat when ordering fabric for curtains or blinds so that you do not get the middle of a formalized pattern cut off.

Pelmet: See Cornice and Valance.

Pull-up curtain: Like a gentler form of festoon blind. Much used in England in the seventeenth century to the late nineteenth century.

Ring-shirr tape: Fabric strip with regular rings and two enclosed cords used for shirring blinds such as the Austrian shade.

Ring tape: Fabric strip with rings used for Roman and Balloon shades or blinds.

Rod pocket: Hem or fabric casing through which a curtain rod is pushed.

Roman shade or blind: A shade or blind that draws up into neat horizontal folds by means of cords threaded through rings attached at regular intervals to the back of the fabric. You can either use rings alone or, on heavier fabrics, attach light battens to keep the folds crisp.

Roman shade or blind

Sash curtains: A flat piece of fabric or curtain panel with rod pockets sewn at the top and

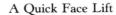

bottom. Ordinary brass or tension rods are then threaded through and mounted at the top and bottom of the window so that the curtain is stretched between them.

Shade: American term for a vertical window covering (also called a blind) which can be rolled up on a spring-roller attachment or drawn up by means of cords threaded through rings.

Shirring: A permanent gathering of fabric achieved by drawing up material along two or more parallel lines of stitching or, more simply, over cords or thin rods that have been threaded through casings or rod pockets.

Slat pocket: The open-ended casing at the bottom hem of a Roman or roller shade through which a rod, batten or wooden slat is passed to add extra weight.

Tie-back: A piece of fabric, cord or chain attached to the window frame and used to loop back curtains or drapes.

Valance: A decorative horizontal panel of fabric usually attached to the top of the window frame or just above it to hide rods and hardware and to provide added interest.

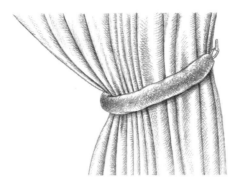

Padded tie-back in matching fabric

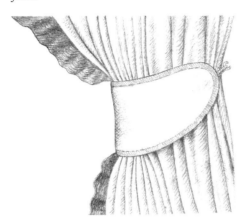

Tasselled cord tie-back

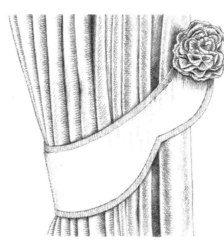

Stiff-lined fabric tie-backs decoratively shaped and with a flower to conceal the fixing

A Quick Face Lift

If you do not want to spend money on new window treatments, it is possible to cheer up existing curtains, drapes or shades quite cheaply.

Long curtains or drapes hanging loose can be given a new look by looping them back with tie-backs made from lengths of cord or from fabric and attached to hooks fixed at the preferred height to the window frame.

You could add a border or binding down the leading and bottom edges of curtains to add a decorator touch. Choose a colour from the existing design or a contrasting colour if the fabric is plain, and add fabric tie-backs to match.

If you are handy with a needle, you could sew in another lining or backing in a contrasting or toning fabric to the front of the curtains, as in the early nineteenth century. Add a print lining to a plain material; a small-scale design in the same colours to a large-scale design; a geometric design in the same colours to a mini-flower pattern. If you then loop the curtains back, you will get glimpses of the new addition, which will make them look more interesting and they should also hang better because of the extra weight.

You could make inner curtains in a sheer fabric or light cotton to hang underneath the old ones, or buy ready-made curtains in a lighter fabric which will tone in with the old ones. These could then be drawn at night and the old ones left looped back to act as a frame. This will add a new dimension to the room and give more perspective to the window.

The same sort of effect can be achieved by tying back the old curtains and adding new blinds or shades. Matchstick blinds are cheap and they could be spray-painted to tone in with the curtain colours or left natural. Alternatively, you could add Venetian, louver, roller, Roman or Austrian shades, depending on your taste.

Old shades can be given a new lease of life in much the same way as curtain and drapes: old matchstick or bamboo blinds can be spray-painted white, black or a colour, and fabric shades can be given a border of a thin material stuck on with Copydex.

213

DIRECTORY OF SOURCES

BRITISH SUPPLIERS

(* denotes trade only. Contact address given for nearest stockist or supplier.)

Furniture and Antiques

Apter Fredericks,
265-267 Fulham Road,
London SW3 6HY
01-352 2188
(18th century furniture)

J&J Baker,
12-14 Water Street,
Lavenham,
Sudbury,
Suffolk
0787 247610
(17th, 18th and 19th century furniture; also watercolours, silver and objets d'art)

Joanna Booth Antiques,
247 Kings Road,
London SW3 5EL
01-352 8998
(Early oak and walnut furniture; 17th and 18th century wood carvings; textiles, braids and tapestries, old master and architectural drawings)

The Dining Room Shop,
64 White Hart Lane, Barnes,
London SW13 0PZ
01-878 1020
(Everything for the dining room, including antique furniture, old and modern cutlery, porcelain, glass and linens)

Harvey Ferry and William Clegg,
The Barn, High Street,
Nettlebed,
Oxfordshire
0491 641533
(17th and 18th century furniture)

Rupert Gentle Antiques,
The Manor House, Milton Lilbourne,
Nr Pewsey, Wiltshire
067 26 3344
(Specialize in 17th and 18th century brass; also 18th century furniture, decorative objects, paintings)

Christoph Gibbs,
118 New Bond Street,
London W1
01-629 2008
(Distinguished and idiosyncratic furniture, paintings, objets d'art and textiles)

Myriad Antiques,
131 Portland Road,
London W11
01-229 1709
(Furniture, decorative objects, kitchen and bathroom accessories)

Page Couts Ltd,
101-107 West Row,
Edinburgh EH1 2JP
031-225 3238
(17th and 18th century furniture; works of art)

Westenholz Antiques,
68 Pimlico Road,
London SW1
01-730 2151
(Idiosyncratic 18th and 19th century furniture of distinction; also interesting objets d'art)

O.F. Wilson Ltd,
Queens Elm Parade, Old Church Street,
London SW3 6EJ
01-352 9554
(Fine decorative furniture, period marble mantelpieces and objets d'art)

Pine

The Pine Mine,
100 Wandsworth Bridge Road,
London SW6
01-737 1092
(Antique pine furniture)

Scallywag,
187-191 Clapham Road,
London SW9 0QE
01-274 0300
(Antique and reproduction furniture; also old doors, fire surrounds, banister rails, panelling, etc.)

Stow Away (UK) Ltd,
2 Langton Hill,
Horncastle,
Lincolnshire LN9 5AH
065 82 7445
(Old pine furniture; specialize in farmhouse kitchen tables; also doors)

Upholstery

Howard Chairs*,
30-31 Lyme Street,
London NW1
01-482 2156
(Sofas and chairs)

G and A Kelly*,
Unit 4,
The Heliport Industrial Estate,
40 Lombard Road,
London SW11
01-228 9812
(Sofas and chairs)

Beds

The Antique Brass Bedstead Company Ltd,
Baddow Antique Centre, Church Street,
Great Baddow, Chelmsford, Essex
0245 71137

(Victorian brass, brass and iron, and iron bedsteads)

Pictures

Philip Mould (Portraits) Ltd,
173 New Bond Street,
London W1
01-491 4627

(Decorative and historical portraits)

Bathroom Fittings

(See also under Architectural Details)

Czech and Speake Ltd,
39c Jermyn Street,
London SW1
01-980 4567

(Good range of Edwardian bathroom fittings; contact them for nearest stockist)

C.P. Hart and Sons Ltd,
Newnham Terrace, Hercules Road,
London SE1 7DR
01-928 5866

(Traditional-style bathroom fittings)

Sitting Pretty,
131 Dawes Road,
London SW6
01-381 0049

(Everything for the bathroom, antique or reproduction; particularly good for decorated Victorian lavatories and basins)

Architectural Details

Architectural Heritage,
Boddington Manor,
Boddington, Nr Cheltenham,
Gloucestershire
024 268 741

(Antique panelling, chimneypieces, stained glass and reproduction Victorian sanitary ware)

The London Architectural Salvage
and Supply Co.,
Mark Street (off Paul Street),
London EC2A 4ER
01-739 0448

(Old fireplaces, panelling, floor boarding and tiles, door furniture, bathroom, kitchen and light fittings)

Walcot Reclamation,
108 Walcot Street,
Bath,
Avon BA1 5BG
0225 66291

(Traditional building materials, period bathrooms, chimneypieces, doors, stained glass, panellings, balustrades)

Fireplaces

Acquisitions,
269 Camden High Street,
London NW1 7BX
01-485 4955

(Antique and reproduction Victorian and Edwardian fireplaces)

Acres Farm Fenders,
Acres Farm,
Bradfield,
Reading,
Berkshire
0734 744305

(Club fenders made to order)

Hollinshead & Co.,
783 Fulham Road,
London SW6
01-736 6991

(Antique and reproduction fireplaces, grates and fenders)

Phoenix Fireplaces,
51 Lark Lane,
Liverpool L17 8UW
051 727 3578

(Antique and reproduction Victorian fireplaces, tiles and furniture)

Door and Window Accessories

Knobs and Knockers,
36-40 York Way,
London N1
01-278 8925

(Traditional Regency, Georgian and Victorian door and window furniture; contact them for nearest stockist or for catalogue)

Locks and Handles,
8 Exhibition Road,
London SW7
01-584 6800

(Traditional designs for locks and handles)

Lighting

Kelly's of Knaresborough,
rear of 96 High Street,
Knaresborough,
Yorkshire
0423 862041

(Large stock of chandeliers, lights, oil lamps, candlesticks of all periods up to 1930)

D.H. Sargent,
21 The Green,
Westerham,
Kent
0959 62130

(Early Georgian to late Victorian lamps, chandeliers and candelabra)

Christopher Wray,
600 King's Road,
London SW6 2DX
01-736 8434

(Original copies of Victorian, Edwardian and Art Nouveau lighting; contact them for nearest showroom or for colour catalogue)

ANTIQUE TEXTILES

Lace

Lunn Antiques,
86 New Kings Road,
Parsons Green,
London SW6
01-228 9812

(Old and new lace tablecloths, cushions, pillows and bedspreads)

Chintzes, Embroideries, Paisleys

The Antique Textile Company,
100 Portland Road,
London W11
01-221 7730

(Regency chintz quilts, toiles de Jovy and printed cottons, cashmere and paisley shawls, oriental textiles, pre-1830 lace, some William Morris and Voysey designs)

The Green Room,
2 Church Street,
Framlinsham,
Woodbridge,
Suffolk
0728 723009

(Specialize in antique textiles but also stock antique furniture, pictures and objets d'art)

215

FABRICS

Revivals

G.P. & J. Baker Ltd*,
West End Road,
High Wycombe,
Bucks HP11 2QD
0494 33422

(*Chintzes and damasks; contact them for nearest supplier*)

Bennison Fabrics Ltd,
91 Pimlico Road,
London SW1
01-730 8076

(*Fabrics made to order, most of them printed on linen*)

Gainborough Silk Weaving Co. Ltd*,
Alexandra Road,
Sudbury,
Suffolk LO10 6AX
0787 72081

(*Good traditional damasks; contact them for nearest supplier*)

Mrs Monro,
11 Montpelier Street,
London SW7
01-589 5052

(*Mainly 19th century chintz designs*)

Ramm, Son and Crocker Ltd*,
13-14 Treadaway Technical Centre,
Treadaway Hill,
Loudwater,
High Wycombe,
Bucks
06285 29373

(*Old chintz designs recoloured*)

Sekers Fabrics Ltd*,
15 Cavendish Place,
London W1
01-636 2612

(*"English country house collection" reproduced from original hand blocks; contact them for nearest supplier*)

George Spencer,
36 Sloane Street,
London SW1
01-235 8131

(*Own range of traditional chintzes*)

Tissunique Ltd*,
10 Princes Street,
Hanover Square,
London W1R 7RD
01-491 3386

(*Fabrics include Barrington Court collection of wool damasks and National Trust collection; contact them for nearest supplier*)

Natural Fabrics

Ian Mankin,
109 Regents Park Road,
Primrose Hill,
London NW1 8LR
01-722 0997

(*Wide range of natural fabrics including ticking, cheesecloth, muslin and dyed or natural cotton*)

FABRICS AND WALLCOVERINGS
(mostly traditional chintzes and wallpapers)

Laura Ashley,
Customer Services, Braywick House,
Braywick Road,
Maidenhead,
Berkshire
0628 39151

(*Printed cottons and wallpapers; also accessories. Contact them for nearest branch or stockist; also available by mail order*)

Colefax and Fowler,
39 Brook Street,
London W1Y 1AN
01-493 2231

(*Contact them for nearest supplier*)

Charles Hammond,
165 Sloane Street,
London SW1
01-235 2151

(*For nearest supplier, contact Pallu and Lake – see below*)

Liberty,
Regent Street,
London W1R 6AH
01-734 1234

(*Contact them for nearest branch or stockist*)

Osborne and Little,
304 Kings Road,
London SW3 5LH
01-352 1456

(*Contact them for nearest branch or stockist*)

Pallu and Lake*,
2a Battersea Park Road,
London SW11

(*Fabrics and wallcoverings include Edith de Lisle collection of updated traditional designs; contact them for nearest stockist*)

Warner & Sons Ltd*,
7-11 Noel Street,
London W1V 4AL
01-439 2411

(*Contact them for nearest supplier*)

Revivals
(Most of above suppliers also include revivals in their range)

Cole and Son,
18 Mortimer Street,
London W1
01-580 2288

(*Wallcoverings*)

Arthur Sanderson and Sons Ltd,
52 Berners Street,
London W1
01-636 7800

(*William Morris fabrics and wallpapers; contact them for nearest stockist*)

Watts and Co. Ltd,
7 Tufton Street,
London SW1 P3QE
01-222 7169

(*Victorian wallpapers made in traditional way using hand blocks; also Victorian woven fabrics*)

Borders and Trimmings

Distinctive Trimmings,
17 Kensington Church Street,
London W8
01-937 6174

(*Cords, braids, tassels and fringes*)

Hill and Knowles,
133 Kew Road,
Richmond, Surrey
01-948 4010

(*Wallpaper and fabric borders*)

Henry Newberry*,
51-53 Mortimer Street,
London W1N 8AU
01-636 5970

(*Cords, braids, tassels and fringes*)

FLOORINGS

Matting

David Douglas (Carpets) Ltd*,
235 Queenstown Road,
London SW8
01-622 1155

(Coia and sisal matting; contact them for nearest supplier)

Waveney Apple Growers,
Common Road,
Aldeby, Nr Beccles,
Suffolk NR34 0BL
050 277 345

(Rush matting; contact them for nearest supplier)

Terracotta Tiles and Bricks

Fired Earth,
102 Portland Road,
London W11
01-221 4825

(A wide range of hand-made terracotta floor tiles; also quarry tiles and Norfolk pamments; they make their own Delftware)

Paris Ceramics,
543 Battersea Park Road,
London SW11
01-228 5785

(Old and reproduction ceramic and terracotta wall and floor tiles)

SALE ROOMS

Christie's,
8 King Street,
London SW1 Y6QT
01-839 9060

(Regular auctions covering all categories of fine and decorative arts, including furniture, textiles, porcelain, pictures and objets d'art; contact King Street for nearest sale room)

Phillips,
7 Blenheim Street,
London W1Y 0AS
01-629 6602

(Regular auctions of furniture, textiles, porcelain, pictures and objets d'art; also kitchen and bathroom fittings in some sale rooms; contact Blenheim Street for nearest sale room)

Sotheby's
34 New Bond Street,
London W1A 2AA
01-493 8080

(Regular sales of furniture, textiles, porcelain, pictures and works of art; contact New Bond Street for nearest sale room)

AMERICAN SUPPLIERS

16th and 17th Century Furnishings

Fallen Oaks Ltd,
1075 Gage Street,
Winnetka,
Ill. 60093
312-446-3540

(Furniture; also textiles)

Vernay & Jussel Inc.,
825 Madison Avenue,
New York, NY 10021
212-879-3344

(Furniture, brass accessories, clocks)

Yeakel Von Eldik & Pruyn,
425 Bia Corta,
Malaga Colve Plaza,
Palos Verdes Estates,
Cal. 90274
213-544-2514

(Furniture, paintings)

18th and 19th Century Furnishings

Don Badertscher Imports,
716 North LaCienga Blvd,
Los Angeles, Cal. 90069
213-655-6448

(19th century furniture)

Bardith Ltd,
901 Madison Avenue,
New York, NY 10021
212-737-3775

(Furniture, accessories)

Mike Bell Antique Showrooms,
60 East 10th Street,
New York, NY 10003
212-598-7099 (and)
12110 Merchandise Mart,
Chicago, Ill. 60654
312-661-7099

(Furniture)

British Country Antiques,
50 Main Street North,
Woodbury,
Conn. 06798
203-262-5100

(Furniture, accessories)

R. Brooke Ltd,
138 1/2 East 80th Street,
New York,
NY 10028
212-535-0707

(Furniture, porcelain, prints)

Bull & Bear Antiques,
1189 Howell Hill Road, N.W.,
Atlanta,
Ga. 30318
404-355-6697

(18th century furniture)

English Heritage Antiques,
13 South Avenue,
New Canaan, Conn. 06840
(Furniture, porcelain)

The English Way
115 East 60th Street,
New York, NY 10022
212-308-6119
(Pine furniture, antique lace, linens, china, accessories)

Rufus Foshee Antiques,
PO Box 839,
Camden, Maine 04843
207-236-2838
(Pottery and porcelain)

Malcom Franklin Inc.,
15 East 57th Street,
New York, NY 10022
212-308-3344
(18th and 19th century furniture, mirrors)

Hamilton-Hyre Ltd,
413 Bleeker Street,
New York, NY 10014
212-989-4509
(Furniture, accessories)

Harwood Galleries,
1045 Madison Avenue,
New York, NY 10021
212-744-5062
(19th century furniture)

Hyde Park Antiques Ltd,
836 Broadway,
New York, NY 10003
212-477-0033
(Formal furniture, mirrors)

Jackson Mitchell Inc.,
412 Delaware Street,
New Castle,
Delaware 19720
302-322-4363
(17th, 18th and 19th century formal and country furniture; 18th and 19th century metalware)

Kensington Place Antiques,
80 East 11th Street,
New York, NY 10003
212-533-7652
(Decorative furniture, objects, prints)

Kentshire Galleries Ltd,
37 East 12 Street,
New York, NY 10003
212-673-6644
(19th century paintings, lighting fixtures)

Linlo House Inc.,
1019 Lexington Avenue,
New York, NY 10021
212-288-1848
(Furniture, lighting fixtures, prints)

Mill House Antiques,
Route 6,
Woodbury, Conn. 06798
(Furniture)

Florian Papp Inc.,
962 Madison Avenue,
New York, NY 10021
212-288-6770
(Furniture, porcelain, clocks, accessories)

Juan-Portela Antiques,
783 Madison Avenue,
New York, NY 10021
212-650-0085
(19th century furniture, English carpets, chairs, antiques, silks, tapestries)

Trevor Potts Antiques Inc.,
1011 Lexington Avenue,
New York, NY 10021
212-737-0909
(Furniture, decorative objects, porcelain, dog paintings, needlework pillows, carpets)

Ralf's Antiques,
807 La Cienga Blvd,
Los Angeles, Cal. 90069
213-659-1966
(Country furniture, paintings, brass accessories)

G. Randall Inc.,
229 N. Royal Street,
Alexandria, Va. 22314
212-549-4432
(Late 17th and 18th century furniture, paintings, mirrors, porcelain)

Stair & Co.,
59 East 57th Street,
New York, NY 10022
212-355-7620
(17th and 18th century furniture, objets d'art)

Stair's Incurable Collector,
42 East 57th Street,
New York,
NY 10022
212-755-0140
(Paintings, English screens, lamps, coffee tables)

Tranquil Corners Antiques,
5634 Chapel Hill Blvd,
Durham,
N.C. 27707
919-489-8362
(Furniture, accessories, silver)

Gene Tyson Inc.,
19 East 69th Street,
New York,
NY 10021
212-744-5785
(18th century furniture, Regency lacquer-gilded pieces, mirrors)

Earle D. Vandekar,
15 East 57th Street,
New York,
NY 10022
212-308-2022
(Ceramics, porcelain, decorative objects)

FABRICS AND WALLCOVERINGS

Cherchez,
864 Lexington Avenue,
New York,
NY 10021
212-737-8215
(Antique table and bed linens, needlepoint pillows, samplers, and paisley throws)

Gilliatt Enterprises English Country Collection,
PO Box 827,
Gracie Station,
New York,
NY 10028
212-348-2370
(Mail order fabrics)

Designer Close-outs, End of Lines, Over-orders

S. Beckenstein Inc.,
130 Orchard Street,
New York
212-475-4525
(Includes Laura Ashley, Schumaker, Greff, Brunschwig)

Calico Corners,
681 East Main Street,
Mount Kisco, West Chester, NY
(Includes Clarence House, Cowtan and Tout, Greff)

Fabricworld Textile Corporation,
283 Grand Street,
New York
212-925-0412
(Damasks, brocades, velvets and prints)

Seaport Fabrics,
Route 27, Mystic,
Connecticut
203-536-8668
(Includes Laura Ashley, Schumaker; canvas duck, corduroy and crewel)

Silk Surplus,
1147 Madison Avenue,
New York, NY 10028
212-794-9373
(Includes Scalamandré fabrics)

Stonehenge Mill Store,
30 Canfield Road Industrial Village,
Cedar Grove,
New Jersey
201-239-9710
(Includes Brunschwig, screen-printed cottons, damasks and tapestries)

Textile Mill End Shop,
57 Garfield Avenue,
East Islip,
Long Island
516-581-9877
(Includes Schumaker, Waverley, 5th Avenue; also linen, wool, crewel, embroideries and cottons)

FLOORING

Tiles

Country Floors,
300 East 61st Street,
New York, NY 10021
212-788-7414

Matting

The Corner Shop*,
360 Decorative Center,
Dallas, Texas 75207

Harmony Carpets*,
D&D Building,
979 Third Avenue,
New York, NY 10022

Sarah Lee Corporation*,
315 National Plaza,
Chicago, Ill. 60602

*(*denotes trade only. Go through a designer or contact Gilliatt Enterprises Inc., 150 East 74th Street, New York, NY 10022, for mail order purchases of designer furnishings.)*

FURTHER READING

Victorian Comfort: A Social History of Design, 1830-1900 by John Gloag (David & Charles, 1973)

The National Trust Book of the English House by Clive Aslet and Alan Powers (Viking, 1985)

English Cottages and Farmhouses by Olive Cook, photographed by Edwin Smith (Thames & Hudson, 1982)

Life in the English Country House by Mark Girouard (Yale University Press, 1978)

The Victorian Country House by Mark Girouard (Oxford University Press, 1971).

The English Country House by Olive Cook (Thames & Hudson, 1984)

The English Country House: A Grand Tour by Gervase Jackson-Stops and James Pipkin (The National Trust/Weidenfeld & Nicolson, 1985)

An Illustrated History of Interior Decoration by Mario Praz (Thames & Hudson, 1982)

English Interiors 1790-1848 by John Cornforth (Barrie & Jenkins)

Authentic Decor: The Domestic Interior, 1620-1920 by Peter Thornton (Weidenfeld & Nicolson, 1984)

The Inspiration of the Past by John Cornforth (Viking, 1985)

The History of Interior Decoration by Charles McCorquodale (Phaidon, 1983)

Below Stairs in the Great Country Houses by Adeline Hartcup (Sidgwick & Jackson, 1980)

Clean and Decent: A History of the Bathroom and the WC by Lawrence Wright (Routledge, 1966)

The English Room by Derry Moore and Michael Pick (Weidenfeld & Nicolson, 1985)

Kitchens and Dining Rooms by Mary Gilliatt (Viking/Orbis, 1983)

A House in the Country by Mary Gilliatt (Hutchinson, 1972)

Bathrooms by Mary Gilliatt (Viking, 1971)

INDEX

Italic numerals indicate illustrations

accessories, *see* objects
Adam, Robert 46, 68, 112, 201, 210
Aldenham Park 68-9
antiques 122
  salerooms 215
  suppliers 214
architectural detail 201
  suppliers 215
arms & armour 38, 49
Arrowsmith: *The Housepainters' and Decorators' Guide* 160
Art Nouveau 167
Ashley, Laura 81, *155*, *158*, 167, 216
Askwith, Betty: *Two Victorian Families* 172
aumbries 139
Avray Wilson, Frank *30*

Bacon, Francis 67, 91
barn *30*, *31*, *73*
baseboard, *see* skirting board
baskets *48*, *54*, *58*, 87, *107*, *128*, *133*, *167*
bath *180*, *181*, *194*, 195, 198, *199*
bathroom 159, 177-199
  bath-dressing room *198*
  converted bedrooms *182*, 196
  suppliers 215
  Victorian *194*
Bauer, Leopold 125
Bauhaus 86
beams *23*, *39*, 51, *54*, 66, *70*, *127*, *148*, *152*, *165*, *191*
bed *146*, *147*, *148*, *149*, *153*, *155*, *158*, *159*, *163*
  bedstead *152*, *153*
  child's *175*
  four-poster *148*, *154*, *211*

hangings 148-9, 154, *158*, *159*, *160*, *162*, *163*, *165*, 211, *211*
  suppliers 215
bedding *147*, *151*, 157, *164*, 165
bedroom 147-195
  accessories 165
  Palladian style 45
  sleeping alcove 154
  suites 159-161
Bennison, Geoffrey 81
billiards table 96
Blenheim Palace 191
blinds & shades *170*, 198, 211-213
  Austrian 81, *176*, *193*, 211, *211*
  balloon 211, *211*
  festoon *170*, *181*, *182*, 211, *211*
  matchstick 213
  Roman 212, *212*
  painted 161, 213
bookcase 77, 93, *94*, 101, *104*, *160*
books 90-91, *91*, *92*, 97
  false spines 95, *95*
  storage of 103
bookshelves *73*, 93, *93*, *99*, 103
  false 95, *95*
  landings 60, 92, 103, *107*
  library *90*, *92*
boudoir *156*, 159
Bramah, Joseph 192
brick: ageing 208-9
  fireplace *68*
  floor *39*, *127*, *131*, *143*, 145, 208, 209
  suppliers 217
  walls *17*, *18*, *21*, *24*, *102*, *133*
Bromley Davenport, Lady: *History of Capesthorne* 84
Buckingham Palace 195
Burlington, Lord 45

Campbell, Colen 48, 68

candelabra *48*, *116*
candles *110*, 123, 127
Carlton House 19
carpet 76
  bedroom 165
  oriental *70*, 74, 110
  table 'carpets' 74, 95
Cassell's *Household Guide* 122, 163
Castle Howard 46
ceilings *42*, *43*
  beamed *23*, *39*, 66, *70*, *127*, *148*, *152*, *165*, *191*
  plaster *43*, 45, 48
  wood *133*
chair rail 48, 87, *121*, 123, *126*, *168*, *180*
chairs *62*, 77, *110*, *111*, *126*, *159*
  dining *116*, *126*
  loose covers 81, *158*
  upholstered *78*, 81
chamber 147
chamber pot 113, *187*, *193*, 197
chandeliers *62*, *115*, *140*
Chatsworth House 84, 95, 191
children's rooms *152*, 171-175, *173*
  bathroom *196*
  furniture 130
  toys *171*
chintz 76, 77, *80*, 81, 89, 101, 122, *146*, *149*, 157, *159*, *163*, *164*, *192*, *195*
  suppliers 215
clapboard *8-9*
cloakroom 117-118, *193*, 199
  see also water closet
clock, longcase *50*, *55*, *63*, *69*, *113*
close-stool *188*, *189*, 197
coats of arms 38, 60
Colefax & Fowler 81, 216

colour: dining rooms *113*, 117, *117*
  furniture 210
  paint 201
  painted floors 206
  studies *95*
commode *177*, *179*, *190*, *197*
Conran, Terence 143
conservatory *27*, *72*, 84, *85*
  marbled wallpaper *84*, 204
Cook, Olive 7
Cornforth, John: *English Interiors* 67
  Inspiration of the Past, 7-10, 11, 201
cornice *44*, *80*, *83*, *90*, *115*, *140*, 211-212
cottage look *39*, *69*, 87, *195*
couch *69*, *92*
  see also sofa
creepers *9*, *18*, *29*
Crozer, Vera 204
Cummings, Alexander 192
cupboard: 'aumbries' 139
  dining room *109*, 110
curtains & draperies 74, 81, 149, 210-213
  bathroom *176*, *185*, *191*, *193*, *195*, 198
  bedroom *146*, *150*, 160-161, *161*, *162*, *164*, *165*, *166*, 170-1
  café 211, *211*
  dining room *114*, *115*, 122, *126*
  hall 38, *62*, 65
  headings 212, *212*
  hourglass 212, *212*
  kitchen *132*
  linings 213
  sash 212-213
  sitting room *80*, 87

tie-back *213*
valance 213
see also bed: hangings; blind; lace; pelmets
cushions *67, 68, 151, 155, 159, 167*

dado *38, 43, 53, 54, 83, 117, 126, 146, 175, 202*
Deepdene 70
desk *103, 161*
see also writing table
dining room 109-127
  book-lined 103
  hall *48*
  lighting 123
Disraeli, Benjamin: *Henrietta Temple* 84
Doddington Park 192
door, entrance 36
  panels, decorated *140, 141*
  suppliers of accessories 215
dragging (paint) *160, 163*, 202-3
draperies, *see* curtains
drawing room *71, 74*
dresser *59, 117, 120, 133, 134, 135, 138, 139, 142, 145*
dressing room 159
dressing table *151, 160*

Edgeworth, Maria 70
Elizabethan hall 42-45
Empire-style cabinet *127*
Erasmus 39

fabrics: bedrooms 157, 158, 163
  shirring 205, *205*, 213
  suppliers 215-216, 218-219
  wall coverings 117, 126, *155*, 204-205, *204, 205*
  see also bed: hangings; chintz; curtains; lace; tapestries
Fabritrack 205
farmhouse *16*
  bathroom *191*
  bedroom *148, 152, 165, 172*
  dining room *110, 114, 119*, 127
  hall *50, 54*
  kitchen *123*, 130-131
  sitting room 66
  study *93*
faucets, *see* taps
fender 98
  club *42, 90*

fireplace *23, 42, 42, 46, 47, 54, 55, 68, 70, 78, 87, 98, 119*, 165, *188, 189*, 199
  brick 68
  kitchen grate *128, 143*
  marble *86, 121, 122*
  medieval 36
  suppliers 215
firescreen *86, 100*
flagstones *31, 44, 45, 55, 59, 61, 63*, 139, 145, 208-209
floor, brick *39*, 127, *131, 143*, 145, 208, 209
  cork *123*
  marble 36, *38, 40*, 108
    faux *207, 207*
  pamments 208
  rush 39
  stone *34*, 108
    flagstone *31, 44, 45, 55, 59, 61, 63*, 139, 145, 208-209
    stone-effect tiles 207
  wood 76, 108, 206
    bleaching 64, *208, 208*
    lightening 208
    painted *84, 145, 173*, 206
    parquet *81*, 127, 208
    sanded *50* 101, *121, 132*, 145, 206, *206*
    stained 207-208, *208*
    stencilled 206, *206*
floorcloth, painted 206-207
flooring, suppliers 217
  see also carpet; matting; rug
floor tiles *84*, 145
  faux *109*, 207, *207*
  quarry 59, *136, 139*, 145, 208, 209
  stone-effect *207, 207*
flowers & plants *27, 31, 37, 46, 71, 72, 75, 89, 115*
Fowler, John 11, 30, 33, 76, 101, 126, *149*, 167, 201
Frederick, Prince of Wales 19
furniture: bedroom *146, 147, 148, 150, 151, 157, 158, 160, 169*
  dining room *109, 110, 112, 113, 114, 116, 117, 121, 124*, 126
  hall *42, 54, 59, 62, 63*, 65
  kitchen *133, 134*, 135, *136, 138, 142*
  library *90, 92, 100, 101*

painting 209-210
  sitting room *68, 69, 73, 76, 77, 79, 80*
  study *93, 95, 102, 103*
  suppliers 214, 217-218
  Victorian *121, 122*

garden *13, 14, 18, 19, 19, 23, 26, 32*
garderobe 187
gatehouse *21*
Georgian colours 201
Girouard, Mark: *Life in the English Country House* 10, 22, 138, 163
glazes (painting) 202
Goldsmith, Oliver 158
Gothic *19*, 49
guéridon 78
guns *51, 55*

Habitat 143
hall *34*, 35-65, *38, 39, 40, 50, 62*
  back hall 59-60, *60, 64*
  Elizabethan 42-45
  hall-library 103, *106*
  living-hall *42, 43, 46, 48, 54, 55*
  medieval 35-42, *35*
  modern 51-2
  Neo-classical 46-8
  Palladian 45-6
Hardwick Hall 91
Harrington, Sir John 188
hats, displaying 41, 53
Hepplewhite, George 193, 210
Hibbard, Shirley: *Rustic Adornments to Homes of Taste* 84
Hoffmann, Josef 125
Hope, Thomas: *Household Furniture and Interior Decoration* 51, 69-70
Houghton Hall 48, 109
Hughes, Robert 27
hutch, *see* dresser

Innes, Jocasta: *Paint Magic* 209

Jackson-Stops, Gervase: *The English Country House* 7, 95
James, Henry 27
Jones, Inigo 45

Kedleston Hall 191
Kent, William 19, 48, 68, 109
Kerr, Robert: *The Gentleman's House* 118, 132, 159-160
kitchen 129-145
  range 140
  stove 141-3
  units 143
Knole (Kent) 18

lace 7, *155, 157, 163*, 212
  curtains 65, *79, 132*
  suppliers 215
lacquering 203
lamps *36, 62, 63, 77, 80*, 136
  shades *74*, 146
Lancaster, Nancy 76
landings 60, 92, 103, *107*
lantern *44*, 62
Leonardo da Vinci 188
Liberty & Co *130*, 216
library 73, 91-9
  hall-library *106*
  library sitting room *90*, 96-99, *100, 101*
lighting: alcove *46, 52*
  dimmer 62, 123
  dining room 123
  electric 123
  hall *36, 43, 46, 54, 62, 63*
  kitchen *144*
  sitting room 89
  study 103
  see also candelabra; candles, etc
loggia *22*
loose covers 81, 158
Loudon, J.C.: *The Suburban Gardener and Villa Companion* 113, 117, 122

Mackintosh, Charles Rennie 125
manor house *14*, 35-36
marble 48
  black 106
  fireplace *86, 121, 122*
  floor 36, *38, 40*, 108
  marbled paper *84*
  marbling 54, 78, *78*, 110, 126, *207, 207*
matting *47, 74, 79, 97, 209, 209*
  coir *43, 60, 93, 106, 110, 163*, 201, *209*
  rush *74*, 76, 101, 110, 127, *150*, 201, 209

suppliers 217, 219
memorabilia 59, *104, 157, 168,
    171*, 198
Middle Ages: hall 35-42
    nostalgia for 48-49
Middleton Park 96
minstrels gallery 42, 45
mirror 78, *83*, 113, 122, *158, 161,
    189, 190, 197*
    hall *38*
    panels 81
Moot Hall 42
Morris, William *159*, 167, *197*
mouldings 117
musical instruments 7, *62, 66, 77*
Muthesius, Hermann 86

National Trust 81
Neo-Classicism 46-48, 114
Neo-Palladian 45-46
Norman style *35*, 35-42
nostalgia 16, 48-49
nursery 171-175, *174*
    see also children's rooms

objects: bathroom *183*
    bedroom 165
    hall 55-59, *57, 64*
    kitchen *132, 136*
    library *95, 101, 102*
    sitting room *74, 75*
O'Neill, Isabel: *The Art of the
    Painted Finish for Furniture
    and Decoration* 209
oriental style *68, 69, 82*
    colours 201
    rugs & carpets *42, 54, 70*, 74,
        100, 101, 110, 158
    wallpaper 81
Orme, Edward: *Essay in
    Transparent Prints* 161
Osborne & Little *176*, 216
Osborne House 196
Osterley House 191

Paine, James 191
paint: & architectural detail 201
    & blinds 161, 213
    colours 201
    dragging *141, 160, 163*, 202-3
    & floors *84, 173*, 206, *206*
    & furniture 130, 209-210
    glazes 202, *202*
    lacquering 203

marbling 54, 78, *78*, 110, 126,
    207, *207*
pictorial *140, 141*
ragging *62, 65, 89, 95, 103, 109,
    110, 121, 122, 139, 203, 203*
stippling *52, 78, 80, 83, 86, 96,
    151, 203, 203*
texture 201-202
stencilling *47, 103, 160, 167,
    168, 169*, 203-204, *204*
wood-graining 78, 110, 126
Palladian style 45-6, 201
panelling *40, 42*, 54, *75, 77,
    78, 78, 87, 108, 109, 112*,
    126, 154, 157, 158,
    188, 196
    faux 101-103, 126
    mirror 81
papier mâché 95, 117, *156, 159*
pastimes: balls & assemblies 20
    billiards *96*
    croquet *23*
    house parties 27
    literature 95
    sport 22
patchwork *74, 75, 111, 152, 159,
    166*
pelmets *37, 79, 80, 164, 192*, 212
Pepys, Samuel 93, 95, 189
Percier, Charles, & Fontaine,
    P.F.L.: *Recueils de
    Décorations Intérieures* 69
petit-point 68
pewter *52*
pictures *51, 78, 92, 98, 105*
    arrangement *49*
    lights 62
    portraits *37, 43, 50, 69, 112*,
        117
    sporting pictures *23, 46, 55*,
        117
    suppliers 215
pilasters *77*
pillows, *see* cushions
pine *109*, 126, *134*
    suppliers 214
plasterwork 45, 117
    polished *145*
plate rack *135*
Pope, Alexander 96
porch *26*, 36
Post-Modernism 49
powder room, *see* cloakroom
Powys, Mrs Libbe 96

Praz, Mario: *An Illustrated History
    of Interior Decoration* 132
Pugin, Augustus *43*

quarry tiles 59, *136, 139*, 145,
    208, *209*
quilts *148*
    patchwork *74, 75, 111, 152,
        159, 166*

radiators *49, 99, 107*
ragging (paint) *62, 65, 89, 95, 103,
    109, 110, 121, 122, 139, 203,
    203*
range, kitchen 140
Regency style: bedroom 157-158
    colours 210
    curtains *161, 166*
    fabric *204*
    furniture *62, 110, 116*
    porch *26*
renovating furniture 209-210
Repton, Humphry: *Fragments* 97
Rey, J.: *The Whole Art of Dining*
    123
Richardson, John 18
Robinson, Sir Thomas 19
room divider *138*
Rosedale Cottage 69
Royal Pavilion, Brighton 195
rugs: hall *52, 60*
    needlework *82, 87, 93*, 101,
        163, 165
    oriental *42*, 54,*61*, 76, *100*, 101,
        158
    rag *172*

Sackville-West, Vita 18
sale rooms 217
screens 36, *70, 81, 94, 108*
    firescreen *86, 100*
    'screens passage' *38, 39, 108*
    window screen 81
Secession School 125
shade, *see* blind
Shakespeare, William 91
shaving table 193
shellacking 210
Sheraton, Thomas 113, 210
shields, heraldic 38-39
shutters *7, 9*, 54, *65, 87, 132*, 149,
    192, 193
sideboard 49, 111, *112*, 113, 126
Simond, Louis 113

Sissinghurst 18
sitting room 66, 67-89
    library sitting room *90*, 96-99,
        100, 101
skirting board 48, *78*, 89, *121,
    123, 163, 192*
Smith, George: *Collection of
    Designs for Household
    Furniture* 117
Soane, Sir John 99
sofa 7, *54*, 67, 68, 76, 77, 78, *79,
    87*, 157
solar *42*, 70, 109
sporting activities 22, *30*
    displaying trophies *46*, 59
spotlights *36*, 62
stabling *20, 28*
stained glass *31, 38*, 198
staircase *36, 37, 38, 39*, 45, *63, 64*
    bookshelves for *60*, 103
    lighting 62
stencilling *47, 103, 160*, 167, 168,
    203-204, *204*
    fabrics *169*
    floors 206, *206*
stippling *52, 78, 80, 83, 86, 96*,
    151, *203, 203*
stone *14, 15, 20, 25*
    faux 45, 54, *207, 207*
    see also floor, stone
stove: Aga *143*
    kitchen 141-143
    wood-burning 55
Strachey, Marjorie 172
study *93*, 99-107
    study-closet 92-93
summer house *18, 19, 23*
suppliers: UK 214-217
    USA 217-219
Surtees, R.S.: *Mr Sponge's
    Sporting Tour* 197
Syon House 112

table: bedside 159
    'carpets' *74*, 95
    dining 110, 126
    kitchen *134*, 135, *136, 139, 143*
    occasional *83*, 111
    Regency *63, 116*
    tablecloths *74*, 111, *125*
    writing *42, 43*
tapestry & hangings *37, 38*, 54,
    71, 74, 78, 110, *115*, 147,
    154, 196, 204

222

taps *181, 186*
television *74, 100*
Tennyson, Lord Alfred 51
Thackeray, William 33
Thornton, Peter: *Authentic Decor* 7, 161
tiles *84, 106, 135, 143, 145*
  bathroom *176, 187, 198*
  suppliers 217, 219
  see also floor tiles
toilet 154-5, 187-91, 197
towel rail, heated *181, 189, 194*
Trollope, Anthony 114
trompe l'oeil 83, 95
Tudor style *21*

upholstery: staplegun 205
  suppliers 214
  upholstered walls 205

urns *82*
  trompe l'oeil 83

Vanbrugh, Sir John 45, 68
varnish: on floors 206, 207
  on glazes 202
  on wallpaper *180*
Victoria, Queen 195-196
Victorian style *38, 121, 122, 178, 194*
view *13, 14, 15, 23*

Wagner, Otto 125
wainscoting 54
Walker, Thomas 123
wall coverings, *see* fabrics; paint; tapestries; wallpaper
wall lights *36, 62*
wallpaper 54, 81, 117

bathroom *180, 189, 191, 192, 197, 198*
bedroom *158, 160, 161*, 167
dining room *125*
flock 117
marbled *84, 204*
rag-rubbed effect *176*
Walpole, Horace 191
Ware, Isaac: *The Complete Book of Architecture* 45, 191
washbasin *178, 186*
washstand *158, 187, 193*, 197
water closet 187-191, 197
Wilde, Oscar 99, 101
window *14, 23, 54, 80, 157*
  fanlight *44*
  French *11, 23, 82, 83, 89*
  leaded *23, 38*
  oeil de boeuf 181

oriel 38
quatrefoil *180*
shutters *54, 65, 87, 132*, 149
stained glass *31*, 60, 198
stone-mullioned *73*
terms 211-213
window seat *40, 79, 116*, 151
windowsill *64, 65, 65, 114*
window treatments 210-213
  see also blinds; curtains
wine cooler 110, 126
withdrawing room 70-76
Woburn Abbey 191
woodcarving *37*, 45, *122*
  renovating 210
Wright, Lawrence: *Clean and decent 178*
writing table *42, 43*
Wyatt, James 68

ACKNOWLEDGMENTS

I am very grateful to all the owners of the houses pictured in this book, who have allowed us to photograph their homes and have put up – most gracefully – with all the disruption that this entails. In particular, I should like to thank Mr and Mrs Frank Avray Wilson; Dr and Mrs J.D. Bailey; Sir Andrew and Lady Buchanan; Mr Francis Burne; Mr and Mrs Mark Burns; Mr and Mrs Richard Burrows; Mr and Mrs Hugh Cavendish; Ms Susan Collier (whose kitchen is pictured on pp. 136-7); Mr and Mrs David Harvey Evers (the interior on p. 84 was designed by Marguerite Evers); The Squire and Mrs Gerard March Phillips de Lisle (whose home is pictured on pp. 13, 20 left, 23, 34, 37, 92 centre, 108, 135 centre, 160); Mrs Pamela Milburne; Mr and Mrs Henry Nevile; Mr and Mrs David Norman; Colonel and Mrs Andrew Parker-Bowles; The Earl and Countess of Suffolk and Berkshire; Mr and Mrs Stuart Taylor; The Hon. and Mrs Robin Warrender; Mr and Mrs Michael Wigan.

Given my peripatetic life-style, I could never have written the text without the unstinting help and research of Sarah Allen and the cheerful patience and perseverance of Jill Roberts and Ellison Poe. I owe them many thanks, as I do David Fordham and Carol McCleeve of Shuckburgh Reynolds for their hard work and sensitivity, and Elisabeth Brayne and Charles Merullo of Orbis, and Ray Roberts of Little, Brown, who have given me so much encouragement and understanding.